GEOGRAPHIA

QUIK-FINDER

NEW YORK CITY

ALL-NEW EDITION

Published by:
GEOGRAPHIA MAP CO., INC.
317 St. Pauls Ave., Jersey City, N.J. 07306
(201) 656-9173 • (212) 695-6585
PRINTERS   PUBLISHERS   MAPMAKERS

PUBLISHED BY:
GEOGRAPHIA MAP CO., INC.
317 St. Pauls Ave., Jersey City, N.J. 07306
201-656-9173 • 212-695-6585
PRINTERS PUBLISHERS MAPMAKERS

CONTENTS

Note to readers: For the most efficient use of this book, first check the Master Index of Points of Interest on pages 8 through 13.

An alphabetical list of the contents will be found on pages 111 and 112.

INTRODUCTION TO NEW YORK CITY

The "Big Apple" is big in many different ways. It contains so much of every facet of American life that an adequate literary or statistical description is next to impossible. Our best efforts will have to be restricted to an overview of this great city.

We believe that the maps, indexes, drawings and other data included in this book form a good foundation of information on how to get around in the city and what to look for.

This guide provides convenient and useful familiarity which the reader will need so as to permit a more joyous and memorable visit — we hope better by far than could be accomplished without the book. Our aim is to provide a workable, simplified handbook that will become a permanent addition to your collectable information about the city as well as a valuable souvenir of your visit.

In 1981, New York City was estimated to have a population of just over 7,400,000. The metropolitan area includes well over 10,000,000 persons, which makes it one of the largest urban areas in the world — perhaps third or fourth largest, but no one really knows (because many big world cities have no clear boundaries).

New York is the largest city in the United States, and is also the leading port — more than 2,000 miles of docks and piers, and served by 180 different shipping lines. As of 1980, at least 56 airlines were using the three international airports, two of which lie within city limits. Kennedy Airport regularly handles over 40 percent of the nation's overseas air travel and over 55 percent of the export-import air tonnage.

The city's transportation facilities are rounded out by five heliports, two major railway terminals, 40 interstate bus lines, and over 300 miles of subway lines.

The "Big Apple's" geography is complex, but is the basic factor behind the city's great advantage over other places. It spreads completely over two islands, part of another one, and continues on to the mainland of New York State.

New York has always been a gateway city — it was founded for that purpose — as a deep-water port at the mouth of the Hudson River. The entire Hudson-Mohawk watershed became New York City's market area by the time of the American Revolution.

But its growth into a world metropolis dates only from 1825, the year the Erie Canal was completed. That engineering feat. opened up the entire Great Lakes-Midwest region to commerce and trade with New York City and Europe.

The city originally occupied a small piece of land at the southern tip of Manhattan Island. In fact, Wall Street is the site of a wall that served as the original town's outer defenses. As the port grew, the population slowly spread to the north and east, onto Long Island. By 1776, the city extended northward only as far as 23rd Street. But 100 years later, it included the whole of Manhattan Island — 12 miles long.

In 1898, the city assumed its present borders by annexing all of Staten Island, and Kings and Queens counties on Long Island. It now has an area of 320 sq. miles.

Visitors or residents in the Tri‑state area surrounding New York City will find Geographia's *Greater New York Regional Road Atlas* a helpful and up-to-date guide to the region's highways, parks and campgrounds.

NEW YORK CITY and Vicinity

Scale in miles
0   5   10

6

INDEX TO COMMUNITIES

MAJOR POINTS OF INTEREST IN NEW YORK CITY

Where they are located; How to get there, and When to go there

Visitors to New York City often find it difficult to choose what they want to visit or see within the time they have.

The number of attractions far exceeds the time available. But on the basis of experience, and through our research, we have tabulated a "primary group" of attractions — points of interest that consistently rank highest among travelers and vacationists. Additionally, there are some points of interest that are of major importance but they are often located out-of-the-way, and therefore are missed, regrettably, by many visitors.

We think it would be helpful to present this primary group of attractions in a special way, with added information, such as location or address, phone numbers and times to visit. But more important, we have keyed these attractions to our transportation maps: A, B, C, and D subway maps, and E, F, and G bus route maps. Also we give page numbers which lead the reader to the proper map on which the point of interest can be found.

African-American Institute, 833 United Nations Plaza and 47 St. (see page 64); open Mon.—Fri. 9-5, Sat. 11-5; free; phone: 949-5666; Buses Nos. 28, 104, 106; see map G.

American Academy of Arts and Letters, Broadway at 155 St. (see page 72); open Tues.—Sun. 1-4; free; phone: 368-5900; Buses 2, 4, 04, 5; maps E and F; Subways 1 to 157 St. (map A) or Subway A or B to 155 St. (map C).

American Geographical Society, Broadway at 155 St. (see page 64); open Mon.— Fri. 9-4; free; phone: 234-8100; Buses 2, 4 or 5 (maps E and F); Subways A or B to 155 St. (map C).

American Museum of Natural History, Central Park West at 81 St. (see page 72) open Oct.—April; donations;,phone: 873-1300; Buses 10 or 11 (maps E and F); Subways AA, B or D (map C).

American Numismatic Society, Broadway and 155 St. (see page 72); open Tues.—Sat. 9-4:30; free; phone: 234-3130; Buses 2, 4 or 5 (maps E and F); Subways A or B to 155 St. (map C)

American Stock Exchange, 86 Trinity Pl. (see page 67); visitors' gallery open 10-3:30 on business days; free; Buses 6 or 8 (maps E and F); Subway E to World Trade Center (map C) or N or RR to Cortlandt St. (map D)

Battery Park, Southern tip of Manhattan. (see page 67); Open 24 hours a day; Buses 1, 6 or 15 (maps E and F); Subway 1 to South Ferry (map A) or 4 or 5 to Bowling Green (map B)

Bowne House, 37-01 Bowne St., Queens. (see page 108). Tues., Sat., & Sun. 2:30-4:30; free; phone: 359-0528; Buses Q13 or Q16; Subway 7 to Main St. (map A).

Bronx Zoo, see New York Zoological Park

Brooklyn Botanic Gardens, Eastern Parkway between Washington and Flatbush Avs., Brooklyn. (see page 106); Oct. 1—May 31; Free; Buses B47 or B49; Subways 2 or 3 to Eastern Parkway (map A)

Brooklyn Museum, Eastern Parkway and Washington Avs., Brooklyn. (see page 106); Donations; phone: 638-5000; Bus B41; Subways 2 or 3 to Eastern Parkway (map A).

Castle Clinton National Monument, In Battery Park. (see page 67); Daily 8:30-4:30; Free; Phone: 344-7220; Bus M1; Subways 4 or 5 to Bowling Green (map B) or 1 to South Ferry (map D).

Center for Inter-American Relations, 680 Park Av. (see page 72); Tues.—Fri. & Holidays, noon-6; Phone: 249-8950; Buses M1, 2, 3, or 4 (maps E and F); Subway 6 to 68th St. (map B).

Central Park, 59 St. to 110 St., 5th Av. to Central Park West. (see page 70); Central Park Zoo at 64th St.; Daily 10-4:30; Free; Buses M1, 2, 3, 4, 5 or 6 (maps E and F); Subways A, B or D to 59th St. (map C).

Chinatown, near Chatham Sq. West of the Bowery. (see page 67); Buses M1, 6 or 15 (maps E or F); Subways E or A to Canal St. (map C); N or RR to Canal St. (map D); 6 (map B).

City Hall, In City Hall Park, Chambers St. and Broadway. (see page 67); Mon.—Fri.; Free; Appointment Only, Phone: 566-5700; Buses M1 or 6 (maps E and F); M22 (map G); Subways 4, 5 or 6 to Brooklyn Bridge (map B); 2 or 3 to Park Pl. (map A).

Cloisters, The, In Fort Tryon Park, 190 St. and Ft. Washington Av. (see page 64); Map 1—Sept. 30; Phone: 923-3700; Bus M4 (maps E and F); Subway A to 190th St. (map C).

Columbia University, Broadway at 116th St. (see page 84) Tours; Phone: 280-2845, ext. 5573; Buses M4 or 5 (maps E and F); Subway 1 to 116th St. (map A).

Coney Island, Brooklyn. (see page106); Bus B36; Subways B, D, F (map C); M, N (map D) to Coney Island.

Conference House, Hyland Blvd., Tottenville, Staten Island. (see page 109) Bus R103; Rapid Transit (SIRT) to Tottenville Station.

Cooper-Hewitt Museum, 2 E 91 St. (see page 72); Phone: 860-6868; Buses M1, 2, 3 or 4 (maps E and F); Subways 4, 5 or 6 to 86 St. (map B).

Dyckman House, 4881 Broadway. (see page 64) Tues.—Sun. 11-5; Free; Bus M100; Subway A to 207 St. and Bway (map C)

Ellis Island, In New York Harbor. (see page 67); Summer, Ferry from Battery Park leaves daily at 9:30, 11:30, 1:30 and 3:30; Bus M1 to South Ferry (map E); Subways 4 or 5 to Bowling Green (map B)

Empire State Building, 350 Fifth Av. (see page 75); Observation Towers Daily 9:30-Midnight; Buses M2, 3, 4, 5 (maps E and F); Subways B, D or F to 34th St. (map C); N or RR to 34th St. (map D)

Federal Hall National Memorial, 28 Wall St.(see page 67); Memorial Day—Labor Day; Daily 9-4:30; Free; Phone: 264-4367; Bus M1 (maps E and F); Subways 2 or 3 to Wall and William Sts. (map A).

Federal Reserve Bank, 33 Liberty St. (see page 67); Mon.—Fri.; Tours by appointment; Phone: 791-6130; Buses M1, 15, 101 or 102 (maps E and F); Subways J or M to Fulton St. (map D).

Fire Department Museum, 110 Church St. (see page 67); Phone: 570-4230; Buses M6 or 10 (maps E and F); Subways A or AA to Chambers St. (map C).

Flushing Meadows-Corona Park, Van Wyck St., Union Tpke. and 111 St., Queens. (see page 108). Hall of Science; Phone: 699-9400; Subway 7 to 111 St. (map A).

Fordham University, 3 rd Av. and Fordham Rd., Bronx. (see page 104): Tours. Phone: 933-2233: Bus Bx12 from 207th St. (map G); Subway No. 4 to Fordham Rd. (map B)

Fraunces Tavern, 54 Pearl St. (see page 67): Mon.—Fri. 10-4: Free: Phone: 425-1776: Buses M1, 101, 102, or 15 (maps E and F): Subways 4 or 5 to Bowling Green (map B)

Frick Collection, 1 E 70 St. (see page 72), Phone 288-0700: Buses M1, 2, 3, 4 (maps E and F) Subway No. 6 to 68 St. (map B).

Garment District, Between 6th and 7th Avs., 34 and 40 Sts. (see page 43); Buses M106 and 16 (map G): Subways 1, 2 or 3 (map A); B, D or F to 34th St. (map C).

Grand Central Terminal, 42nd St. between Lexington and Vanderbilt Avs. (see page 44); Buses M104, 101 and 102 (maps E, F and G): Subways 4, 5, 6 or 7 to Grand Central (maps A and B).

Greenwich Village, 14 St. South to Houston St., Washington Sq. West to the Hudson River. (see page 36); Buses M2, 3, 5, 6 and 10 (maps E and F) Subways A, B, D or F to West 4th St. (map C).

Hall of Fame for Great Americans, 181 St. and University Av., Bronx. (see page 106): Open Daily 9-5: Free: Buses Bx12 from 207th St. (map G); Subway 4 to Burnside Av. (map B).

Hayden Planetarium, 81 St. and Central Park West (see page 72): Phone: 873-8828: Buses M7 or 10 (maps E and F): Subways 1 to 79 St—Bway (map A); AA to 81st St. (map C).

Hispanic Society of America, Broadway between 155 and 156 Sts. (see page 72): Tues.—Sat. 10-4:30: Sun. 1-4: Free: Phone: 690-0743: Buses M4, 5, 100, 101 maps E and F): Subways 1 to 157 St. (map A): A, AA or B to 155th St. (map C).

John F. Kennedy International Airport, at Junction of Van Wyck Expressway and Belt Parkway, Queens. (see page 50): Subway JFK EXPRESS from 34, 42 or 50th Streets to Howard Beach, and Shuttle bus to airport (map C); Subways E or F to Union Turnpike, Kew Gardens Stations or E or F, and Q10 bus to airport (map C).

John Street Church (United Methodist), 44 John St. (see page 67): Mon.—Fri. 9:30-5: Phone: 269-0014: Buses M1 or 6 (maps E and F); Subways J or M to Fulton St. (map D).

Jewish Museum, 1109 Fifth Av. at 92nd St. (see page 72): Mon.—Thurs. Noon-5, Sun. 11-6: Phone: 860-1888: Buses M1, 2, 3 or 4 (maps E and F); Subway No. 6 to 96 St.—Lex. Av. (map B).

Julliard School, at Lincoln Center for the Performing Arts. (see page 64): Buses M5 and 7 (maps E and F): M29 or 30 (map G): Subway No. 1 to 66 St.—Bway (map A).

Kodak Gallery and Photo Information Center, 1113 Av. of Americas at 43 St. (see page 64): Mon. Noon-5, Tues.—Sat. 9:30-5: Free: Phone: 262-6170: Buses M6, 7, 10 or 104 (maps E and F); M106 (map G) Subways B, D, F to 42nd St. (map C).

LaGuardia Airport, Grand Central Parkway and Flushing Bay, Queens. (see page 51): Subway No. 7 to Main St., Flushing or 111 St., then Bus 48: Subways E, F, N to 74 St.—Bway, then Bus 33.

Lefferts Homestead, In Prospect Park, Flatbush Av, Brooklyn. (see page 106) Nov. 1—may 31; Mon., Wed., Fri., Sat. and Sun. 1-5; Closed Second Sat. of month; Free; Phone: 566-7577; Busway D or M to Prospect Park (maps C and D).

Lincoln Center for the Performing Arts, Broadway at 64 St. (see page 64) Tours Daily 10:30-5; Phone: 874-4012/4010; Bus M5; Subway No. 1 to 66 St.—Bway; see Julliard School.

Madison Square Garden Center, between 7th and 8th Avs., 31 and 33 Sts. (see page 64); Ticket Information Phone: 564-4400; Buses M4 and 10 (maps E and F), M16 (map G); Subways 1, 2, 3 to 34 St. (map A); A, B, D, E, F (map C).

Metropolitan Museum of Art, 5th Av. and 82nd St. (see page 71) Donations; Phone: 535-7710; Buses M1, 2, 3 or 4 (maps E and F); Subways 4, 5 or 6 to 86th St.—Lex. Av. (map B).

Mill, The, Burlington House, 54 St. and Av. of Americas. (see page 64); Tues.—Sat. 10-6 (10-7 in Summer); Free; Phone: 333-3622; Buses M5 and 6 (maps E and F); Subways B, D, F to 50th St. (map C).

Morris-Jumel Mansion, Jumel Terr. at W 161 St. (see page 64); Open Tues.—Sun. 10-4; Phone: 923-8008; Buses M3 or 4 (maps E and F); Subway No. 1 to 157 St. (map A).

Museum of Modern Art, 11 W 53 St. (see page 72); Mon., Tues., and Fri.—Sun. 11-6, Thurs. 11-9; Phone: 956-6100; Buses and subways: same as for Museum of American Folk Art.

Museum of the American Indian Heye Foundation, Broadway between 155 and 156 Sts. (see page 72); Tues.—Sun. 1-5; Phone: 283-2420; see the entry for Amer. Numismatic Soc.

Museum of the City of New York, 5th Av. and 103 to 104 Sts. (see page 72); Tues.—Sat. 10-5, Sun. and holidays 1-5; Free; Phone: 534-1672; Buses M1, 2, 3 or 4 (maps E and F); Subway No. 6 to 103 St. (map B).

New York Aquarium, In Coney Island at West 8th St., Brooklyn (see page 106); Open Daily 10-6; May 30—Labor Day; Phone: 566-7577; Subways B, D, F, N or M to Stillwell Av. or W. 8th St.   (maps C and D).

New York Botanic Garden (in Bronx Park), East Bronx (see page 105); Open Tues.—Sun. 10-4; Subways 2 and 5 to Pelham Pkwy. (maps A and B; D to Bedford Pk. Blvd. (map C).

New York Coliseum, Columbus Circle, 60 St. & 8th Av. (see page 64); For ticket info., call 757-5000; Buses 10, 103, and 30 (maps F and G); Subways 1, 2, or 3 to 59 St. (map A); A, AA, B, D to 59 St. (map C).

New York Historical Society, Central Pk. West at 77 St. (see page 72) Open Tues.—Fri. 11-5; Sat. 10-5; Sun. 1-5; Free (Library costs one dollar); Phone: 873-3400; Bus 10 (map E and F); Subway 1 to 79 St. (map A).

New York Public Library, 42 St. and 5 Av. (see page 64); Open Mon., Wed., Fri. and Sat. 10-6; Tues. 10-9; Phone: 790-6161; Buses 104, 1, 2, 3, 4 (maps E and F); Subways B, D, and F to 42 St. (map C).

New York Stock Exchange, 20 Broad St. (see page 67); Free tours on business days; visitors gallery open 10-3:30; Free; Buses 1, 6 and 15 (maps E and F); Subways 4 or 5 to Wall St. (map B); Subway J to Broad St. (map D)

New York Zoological Park (Bronx Zoo), between Fordham Rd. and Southern Blvd. East Bronx (see page 105). Open Feb.—Sept. 10-5; rest of year 10-4:30; admission $1.50; Subways 2 and 5 to E 180 St. (maps A and B).

Old Merchant's House, 29 East 4 St. (see page 72) Buses 2, 3 or 5 (maps E and F) Subways A, AA, B, D, E or F, to West 4 St. (map C)

Pan American Building, Atop Grand Central Station. at 42-45 Sts. (see page 75) For transportation see Grand Central Station.

Park Avenue, between 46 and 60 Sts.; Bus 30 (map G); Buses 101, 102, 32 (maps E and F); Subways 4, 5 or 6 to 42 St. or 51 St. (map B).

Pierpont Morgan Library, 29 East 36 St. (see page 64). Open Tues.—Sat. 10:30-5 Sun. 1-5 (Sept. 1—June 30); no Sun. in July; Donations; Phone: 685-0008 Buses 1, 2, 3, 4 of 5 (maps E and F); Subway 6 to 33 St. (map B).

Edgar Allen Poe Cottage, Kingsbridge Rd. at Grand Concourse, West Bronx (see page 104) Open Wed., Fri., Sun. 1-5; Sat. 10-4; 50¢; Phone: 881-8900; Subway I to Kingsbridge Rd. (map C).

Police Academy Museum, 235 East 20 St. (see page 72). Open Mon.—Fri. 8-4 Phone: 477-9700; Bus 26 (map G); Buses 16, 101, 102 (maps E and F); Subway 6 to 23 St. (map B).

Prospect Park, at Flatbush Ave. and Grand Army Plaza, Brooklyn (see page 106) Open dawn to dusk; for transportation info., see above at Lefferts Homestead.

Queens Museum, Flushing Meadow Pk., Queens; located in the New York City Building; Open April—Sept., Tues.—Sat. 10-5 and Sun. 1-5; rest of year open Tues.—Sat. 10-5, Sun. 12-4; donations; Phone: 592-2405; for Transportation info., see above at Flushing Meadows Corona Park.

R.C.A. Building, at 30 Rockefeller Plaza. *See* Rockefeller Center.

Riverside Church (interdenominational), Riverside Dr. and 122 St. (see page 102) Bell tower open Mon.—Sat. 11-3; Sun. 12:30-4; 25¢ Phone: 749-7000; Bus 5 (maps E and F); Subway 1 to 125 St. (map A).

Rockefeller Center, from 5 Av. to Ave. of the Americas, 48 to 52 Sts. (see page 78) Hour-long tours leave R.C.A. Building Mon.—Sat. 10-4:45; $2.50; Phone 489-2947; Subway B, D, F to 47-50 St. (map C)

St. John the Divine, Cathedral of, (Episcopal), 1047 Amsterdam Av. (see page 102) Daily 7:15-5; Tours; Phone: 678-6922   Buses M4, 5, 10 or 11 (maps E and F) Subway 1 to 110 St.—Cathedral Pkway (map A).

Saint John's Episcopal Church, 9818 Fort Hamilton Pkwy., Brooklyn (see page 102) Open 24 hours; Subways RR to 95 St.—Ft. Hamilton (map D).

Saint Marks in the Bowery Church (Episcopal), 2 Av. and 10 St. (see page 102) Open Mon.—Fri. 9:30-5; Phone: 673-9402; Buses 101, 102 (maps E and F) Bus 13 (map G) Subway 6 to Astor Place (map B).

Saint Patrick's Cathedral, 5 Av. at 50 St. (see page 102) Open Daily 6 AM-8:30 PM Buses 1, 2, 3, 4 (maps E and F); Subway B, D, or F to 47-50 St. (map C).

Saint Paul's Chapel (Episcopal), Trinity Parish, Broadway at Fulton St. (see page 102); Open daily 7-4; Phone: 732-5564; Buses 10 and 6 (maps E and F) Subways A, 2, 3, 4, 5, 6 (maps A, B and C).

Shea Stadium, Willets Pt., near Flushing Meadows Park. Queens (see page 98) for transportation info. see Flushing Meadows-Corona Pk.

Solomon R. Guggenheim Museum, 5 Av. at 89 St. (see page 72); open Tues. 11-8; Wed.—Sun. and holidays 11-5; $1.50; Phone: 860-1300; for transportation info., see Cooper-Hewitt Museum.

South Street Seaport Museum and Restoration area, start at 16 Fulton St. (see page 67); Open daily 11-6; Closed on major holidays; Phone 766-9020; for Buses, see St. Paul's Chapel; Subways 2 or 3 to Fulton St. (map A).

Staten Island Historical Society Museum, Court and Center Sts. (see page 109); Reach Staten Island via Verrazano Bridge by car or by Staten Island Ferry; For ferry, take buses 1 and 6 (maps E and F) or Subways 1, 4 and 5 (maps A and B); in Staten Island (at St. George), take Bus R4.

Staten Island Institute of the Arts, Stuyvesant Place and Wall St., in St. George (see page 109; Free; Open Tues.—Sat. 11-5; Sun. 2-5; Closed major holidays; Phone: 727-1135; Reach by Staten Island Ferry (see entry above).

Staten Island Zoo, in Barrett Park, Staten Island (614 Broadway, Staten Island) (see page 109); Open daily 10-4 :45; 75¢; Free on Wed.; Closed major holidays; Phone: 442-3100; For transportation info., see entries above; Bus 107 on Staten Island.

Statue of Liberty National Monument, on Liberty Island (see page 67); Ferry boat leaves South ferry at Battery Pk.; $1.50; Phone: 269-5755; Subway 1 to South Ferry (map A) or 4 or 5 to Bowling Green (map B).

Temple Emanu-El, 5 Av. and 65 St. (see page 102); open Sunday—Fri., and holidays 10-5; Closed on High Holy Days; Free; Phone: 744-1400; Buses 1, 2, 3, 4 (maps E and F); Subway 6 to 68 St. (map B).

Theodore Roosevelt Birthplace, 28 East 20 St. (see page 64); Open daily 9-4:30 Memorial Day and Labor Day; closed Mon., Tues. rest of year; 50¢; Phone: 264-8711; Buses 2 or 3 (maps E and F); Subway RR to 23 St. (map D).

Trinity Church (Episcopal), Broadway at Wall St. (see page 102); Open Mon.—Fri. 7-6; Sat., Sun., Hol. 7-4; Phone: 285-0800; Buses 1, 6, or 10 (maps E and F); Subways 4, 5 or 6 to Wall St. (map B).

United Nations Headquarters, First Av. between 42 and 48 Sts. (see page 64) Open daily 9-4:45; one-hour guided tours every ten minutes daily; $2.00; Phone: 754-7710; For transportation info., see African-American Institute.

Van Cortlandt House, Broadway and 264 St., in Van Cortlandt Pk., Bronx. (see page 104); Open Tues.—Sat. 10-5; Sun. 2-5; Phone— 543-3344; Subway 1 to Van Cortlandt Pk (map A).

Wall Street. For transportation info., see Trinity Church.

Washington Square, Greenwich Village, at foot of 5 Av. See information for Greenwich Village.

Whitney Museum of American Art, 945 Madison Av. (see page 72) Open Tues.-- Sat. 11-6; Sun. noon-6; $1.50; Phone: 794-0600; Buses 1, 2, 3 or 4 (maps E and F); Subway 6 to 77 St. (map B).

World Trade Center, Church St. between Vesey and Liberty; Observation deck on 107 floor, promenade 110 floor; deck open daily 9:30-9:30; promenade closed during high winds; $1.70; Buses 10 and 22 (maps E, F, and G); Subway 1 to Cortlandt St. (map A); A, AA, E to Chambers St. (map C).   See page 75

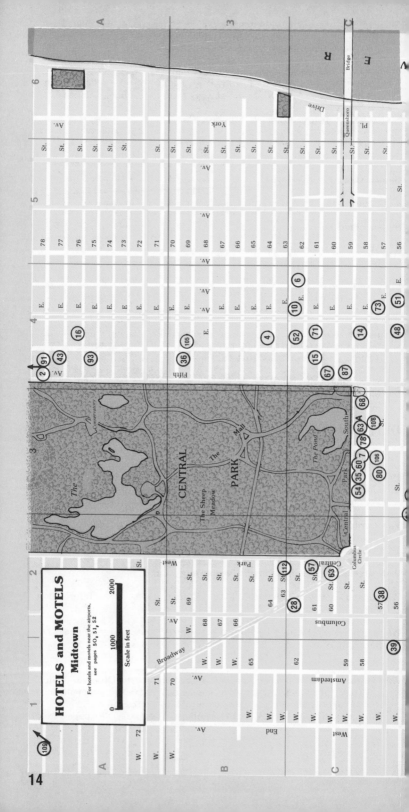

HOTELS and MOTELS
Midtown

For hotels and motels near the airports,
see pages 50, 51, 52

Scale in feet

0   1000   2000

CENTRAL PARK

The Sheep Meadow

The Mall

The Pond

14

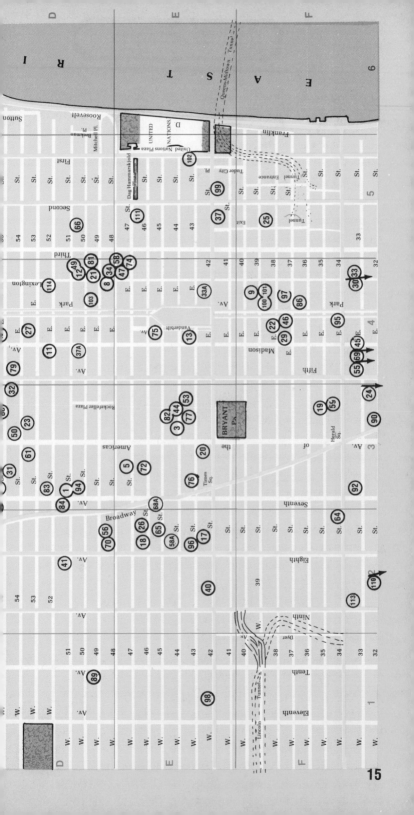

HOTELS and MOTELS

(For Hotels and Motels near the Airports, see pages 50—52)

Map Number   Map Ke

1   **Abbey Victoria,** 7th Av & 51 St; 1000 rooms;
    246-9400; toll free 800-223-5596 . . . . **D-3**
2   **Adams,** 2 E 86 St; 350 rooms; 744-1800 . . . . **A-4**
3   **Algonquin,** 59 W 44 St; 200 rooms;
    840-6800; toll free 800-323-2776 . . . . **E-3**
4   **Alrae,** 37 E 64 St; 246 rooms; 744-0200 . . . . **B-4**
5   **Ashley,** 157 W 47 St; 245-6090 . . . . **E-3**
6   **Barbizon, The** (Women Guests Only), 140 E 63 St;
    650 rooms; 838-5700 . . . . **C-4**
7   **Barbizon-Plaza,** 106 Central Park S; 800 rooms;
    247-7000; toll free 800-223-5493 . . . . **C-3**

8   **Barclay,** 111 E 48 St; 800 rooms; 755-5900;
    toll free 800-221-2690 . . . . **D-4**
9   **Bedford,** 118 E 40 St; 200 rooms; 697-4800 . . . . **F-4**
10 **Beekman,** 575 Park Av, 351 rooms; 838-4900 . . . . **C-4**
11 **Berkshire,** 21 E 52 St; 500 rooms; 753-5800;
    toll free 800-323-1776 . . . . **D-4**
12 **Beverly,** 125 E 50 St; 300 rooms; 753-2700 . . . . **D-4**
13 **Biltmore,** Madison Av & 43 St; 900 rooms; 687-7000;
    toll free 800-221-2690 . . . . **E-4**
14 **Blackstone,** 50 E 58 St; 200 rooms; 355-4200 . . . . **C-4**

15 **Carlton House,** 680 Madison Ave; 400 rooms; 838-3000 . . . . **C-4**
16 **Carlyle,** 35 E 76 St; 500 rooms; 744-1600 . . . . **A-4**
17 **Carter,** 250 W 43 St; 700 rooms; 944-6000 ;
    toll free 800-323-1776 . . . . **E-2**
18 **Century-Paramount,** 235 W 46 St; 700 rooms;
    246-5500; toll free 800-323-1776 . . . . **E-2**
19 **Collingwood,** 45 W 35 St; 200 rooms; 947-2500 . . . . **F-3**
20 **Diplomat,** 108 W 43 St; 921-5666 . . . . **E-3**
21 **Doral Inn,** 541 Lexington Av; 645 rooms;
    755-1200; toll free 800-223-5823 . . . . **D-4**

22 **Doral Park Av,** 70 Park Av; 204 rooms; 687-7050 . . . . **F-4**
23 **Dorset,** 30 W 54 St; 428 rooms; 247-7300 . . . . **D-3**
24 **Earle,** 103 Waverly Place; 200 rooms; 777-9515,
    (located off map in Greenwich Village) **F-3**
25 **Eastgate Tower Motor Inn,** 222 E 39 St; 120 rooms;
    687-8000 . . . . **F-5**
26 **Edison,** 228 W 47 St; 1000 rooms; 246-5000;
    toll free 800-327-3384 . . . . **E-2**
27 **Elysee,** 60 E 54 St; 110 rooms; 753-1066 . . . . **D-4**
28 **Empire,** 1889 Broadway, 600 rooms; 265-7400;
    toll free 800-323-1776 . . . . **C-2**

16

29	**Executive,** 237 Madison Av; 150 rooms; 686-0300	F-4
30	**George Washington,** 23 St & Lexington Av; 600 rooms; 475-1920; toll free 800-323-1776. (located off map at Gramercy Park)	F-4
31	**Gorham,** 136 W 55 St; 185 rooms; 245-1800	D-3
32	**Gotham,** 700 5th Av; 352 rooms; 247-2200; toll free 212-640-4296	D-3
33	**Gramercy Park,** 21 St & Lexington Av; 507 rooms; 475-4320; toll free 800-221-5130; (located off map at Gramercy Pk)	F-4
33A	**Grand Hyatt,** Park Av at Grand Central; 1,400 rooms; 883-1234	E4
34	**Halloran House,** 641 Lexington Av; 650 rooms; 755-4000; toll free 800-645-2000	D-4
35	**Hampshire House,** 150 Central Park S; 510 rooms; 246-7700	C-3
36	**Hampton House,** 28 E 70 St; 92 rooms; 288-2700	B-4
37	**Harley House,** 212 E42 St; 800 rooms; 490-8900	E-5
37A	**Helmsley Palace,** 455 Madison Av; 947 rooms; 888-7000	D4
38	**Henry Hudson,** 353 W 57 St; 265-6100	C-2
39	**Holiday Inn-Coliseum,** 440 W 57 St; 603 rooms; 581-8100	C-1
40	**Holland House,** 351 W 42 St; 400 rooms; 246-0700	E-2
41	**Howard Johnson's Motor Lodge,** 8th Av & 51 St; 300 rooms; 581-4100; toll free 800-654-2000	D-2
43	**Hyde Park,** 25 E 77; 284 rooms; 744-4300	A-4
44	**Iroquis,** 49 W 44 St; 840-3080	E-3
45	**Kenmore Hall,** 145 E 23 St; 475-3840; (located off map)	F-4
46	**Kitano,** 66 Park Av; 112 rooms; 685-0022	F-4
47	**Lexington,** 511 Lexington Av; 800 rooms; 755-4400; toll free 800-228-5151	E-4
48	**Loews Drake,** 440 Park Av; 700 rooms; 421-0900; toll free 800-323-1776	C-4
49	**Loews Summit,** Lexington Av & 51 St; 800 rooms; 752-7000; toll free 800-323-1776	D-4
50	**Loews Warwick,** 65 W 54 St; 425 rooms; 247-2700	D-3
51	**Lombardy,** 111 E 56 St; 400 rooms; 753-8600	C-4
52	**Lowell, The,** 28 E 63 St; 135 rooms; 838-1400	C-4
53	**Mansfield,** 12 W 44 St; 944-6050	E-3
54	**Marriott's Essex House,** 160 Central Park S; 860 rooms; 247-0300; toll free 800-228-9290	C-3
55	**Martha Washington,** (Women Guests Only), 451 rooms; 29 E29 St; 689-1900; (located off map)	F-4
56	**Mayfair,** 240 W 49 St; 426 rooms; 247-1150	D-2

18

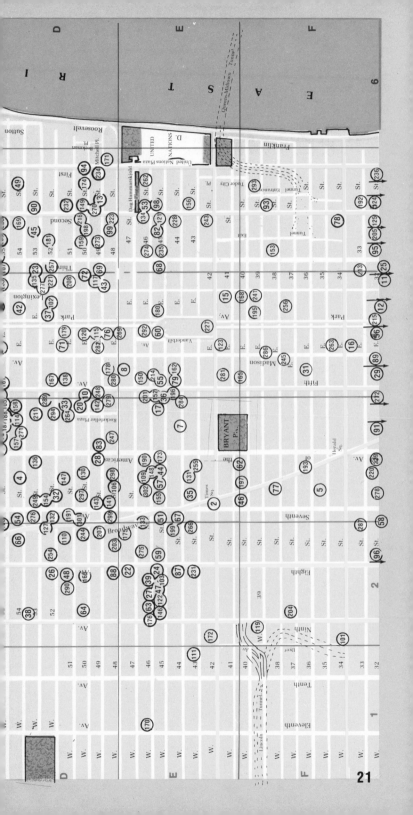

Map Number		Map Key
1	**Abruzzi,** 37 W 56 St: 489-8110: Italian.	C-3
2	**Act I,** One Times Square: 695-1880; American-Continental.	E-3
3	**Akbar India,** 475 Park Av: 838-1717; Asian-Indian	C-4
4	**Al & Dick's Steak House,** 151 W 54 St: 757-0095.	D-3
5	**Al Cooper's,** 130 W 36 St: 244-2828; American	F-3
6	**Alfredo,** 240 Central Park S: 246-7050; Italian	C-3
7	**Algonquin,** 59 W 44 St; 840-6800; Continental.	E-3
8	**Amalfi,** 16 E 48 St: 758-5110; 759-9640; Italian.	D-4
9	**Ambrosia,** 115 E 60 St: 838-6662; Continental.	C-4
10	**American Cafeteria,** 630 5th Av; 581-3580; American.	D-4
11	**Amy's,** 210 E 23 St; 889-2720; Middle East (Located off map).	F-5
12	**Annapurna Indian,** 108 Lexington Av: 679-1284; Indian (Located off map).	F-4
13	**Antolotti's,** 337 E 49 St: 688-6767: Italian.	D-5
14	**Aperitivo,** 29 W 56 St: 765-5155; Italian.	C-4
15	**Applause,** 360 Lexington Av; 687-7267; American.	E-4
16	**Ararat,** 4 E 36 St: 686-4622; Armenian & Middle East.	F-4
17	**Argentine Pavillion,** 30 W 46 St; 921-0835; Argentine	E-4
18	**Arirang House,** 28 W 56 St: 581-9698; Korean.	C-4
19	**Arthur's,** 44 W 56 St: 581-9765; American-Continental.	C-3
20	**Assembly Steak House,** 16 W 51 St; 581-3580	D-4
21	**Autopub,** 767 5th Av: 832-3232; Continental.	C-4
22	**Autunnel,** 306 W 48 St: 582-2166; French.	D-2
23	**Avgerino's,** 153 E 53 St: 688-8828; Greek.	D-5
24	**Backstage,** 318 W 45 St; 581-8447; Continental	E-2
25	**Balkan Armenian,** 129 E 27 St; 689-7925; Armenian (Located off map).	F-5
26	**Bangkok Cuisine,** 885 8th Av: 581-6370; Thai.	D-2
27	**Barbetta,** 321 W 46 St: 246-9171; Northern Italian	E-2
28	**Beanstalk,** 1221 Ave of Americas: 354-4670	D-
29	**Beefsteak Charlie's,** 55 5th Av: 675-4720 (Located off map).	F-
30	**Benihana of Tokyo,** 120 E 56 St: 593-1627; Japanese	C-
31	**Bienvenue,** 21 E 36 St: 684-0215; French.	F-
32	**Bill Hong's,** 133 W 52 St: 581-6730; Chinese-Cantonese.	D-
33	**Bombay Palace,** 30 W 52 St: 541-7777; Indian.	D-
34	**Boodles,** 1478 1st Av; 628-0900; Continental.	A-
35	**Boss,** 1500 Broadway: 997-1830; American.	E-
36	**Brasilia,** 7 W 45 St: 869-9200; Brazilian.	E-
37	**Brasserie,** 100 E 53 St: 751-4840; French-Alsatian.	D-
38	**Brittany Du Soir,** 800 9th Av: 265-4820; French.	D-
39	**Broadway Joe Steak House,** 315 W 46 St: 246-6513.	E-
40	**Bruce Ho's Four Seas,** 116 E 57 St: 753-2610; Cantonese.	C-
41	**Bruno,** 240 E 58 St: 688-4190; Italian.	C-
42	**Brussels,** 115 E 54 St: 758-0457; French.	D-
43	**Bull and Bear, (Waldorf Astoria);** Lexington Av & 49 St: 872-4900; English.	D-
44	**Cabana Carioca,** 123 W 45 St: 581-8088; Brazilian-Portuguese.	E-
45	**Cafe Argenteuil,** 253 E 52 St: 753-9273; French.	D-

22

23

25

RESTAURANTS
Greenwich Village, East Village and Chelsea

The West Side Highway (an elevated, limited access roadway) has been closed to all traffic for an indefinite period, pending completion of plans to reconstruct and reroute the highway. West Street and Twelfth Ave. can both be used for through traffic.

Scale
0   ¼
Miles

29

RESTAURANTS
GREENWICH VILLAGE

Map Number   **Map Ke**

30

RESTAURANTS
Chinatown, Soho
and the
Financial District

Scale in feet   0   500   1000

RESTAURANTS
LOWER MANHATTAN SOHO and CHINATOWN

Number on map	Name and Address · Phone	Map key
1	**Angelo of Mulberry St,** 146 Mulberry St; 966-1277; Italian	B-3
2	**Bernstein-On-Essex St,** 135 Essex St; 473-3900; Jewish Delicatessen	A-4
3	**Bo Bo,** 20 ½ Pell St; 962-9458; Chinese	B-3
4	**Bull and Bear,** 90 West St; 962-0670; English	D-1
5	**Delmonico,** 56 Beaver St; 269-1180; American	E-2
6	**Esther Eng,** 18 Pell St; 732-0175; Chinese	B-4
7	**Ferrara Foods & Confections,** 195 Grand St; 226-6150; Italian Coffee House	B-3
8	**Forlini's,** 93 Baxter St; 349-6779; Italian	B-3
9	**Four Five Six,** 2 Bowery; 964-5853; Chinese	C-4
10	**Fraunces Tavern,** 54 Pearl St; 269-0144; American	E-2
11	**Giambone's,** 42 Mulberry St; 285-1277, 962-8187; Italian	B-3
12	**Giovanni's Atrium,** 100 Washington St; 344-3777; Roman-Italian	E-1
13	**Grotta Azzurra Inn,** 387 Broome St; 226-9283, 925-8775; Italian	A-4
14	**Hee Seung Fung Teahouse,** 46 Bowery; 374-1319; Southern Chinese	C-4
15	**Hwa Yuan Szechaun Inn,** 40 East Broadway; 966-5534; Chinese	C-4
16	**Il Cortile,** 125 Mulberry St; 226-6060; Italian	B-3
17	**Joy Garden,** 48 Mott St; 962-9787; Chinese	B-3
18	**Kabuki,** 115 Broadway; 962-4677/4645; Japanese	D-2
19	**La Crepe,** 59 Nassau St; 732-8680; French	D-2
20	**Mandarin Inn,** 14 Mott St; 962-5830; Northern Chinese	C-4
21	**Market Dining Rooms and Bar,** 1 World Trade Center; 938-1155	D-1
22	**Michael One,** 25 Trinity Pl.; 344-7270; Continental	E-2
23	**Osteria Romana,** 174 Grand St; 925-8540; Italian	B-3
24	**Patrissy's,** 98 Kenmare St; 226-8509; Italian	A-3
25	**Pier Nine,** 149 2nd Av; 673-9263; Seafood-American-Oriental	A-4
26	**Ponte's,** 39 Desbroses St; 226-4621; American-Italian	A-1
27	**Quon Luck Diner,** 66 Mott St; 226-4675; Cantonese	B-3
28	**Raoul's,** 180 Prince St; 966-3518	A-1
29	**Ratners Dairy Restaurant,** 138 Delancey St; 677-5588	A-4
30	**Ruggero,** 194 Grand St; 925-1340; Italian	B-3
31	**Soho Charcuterie,** 195 Spring St; 226-3545; French	A-1
32	**Soho Robata,** 143 Spring St; 431-3993; Japanese	A-2
33	**Spring Street Natural Restaurant;** 149 Spring St; 966-0290	A-2
34	**Sweets,** 2 Fulton St; 825-9786; Seafood	D-3
35	**Szechaun Taste,** 23 Chatham Sq.; 267-0672; Chinese	C-4
36	**Temple Garden,** 16 Pell St; 233-5544; Chinese	B-3
37	**Thomas St. Inn,** 8 Thomas St; 349-6350; Italian-American	C-2
38	**Tung Sing,** 6 E Broadway; 966-0510; Chinese; (Pastry & Supermarket)	C-4
39	**Umberto's Clam House,** 129 Mulberry St; 431-7545	B-3
40	**Windows on the World,** 1 World Trade Center; 938-1111; Continental	D-2
41	**WPA,** 152 Spring St; 226-3444; American	A-2

For restaurants in midtown and Greenwich Village, see pages 20-31

MORE RESTAURANTS
Manhattan

Because of space limitations, we are unable to locate on the maps a large group of other famous restaurants. They are located all around Manhattan. To find out where they are and how to get there, we suggest you consult Maps "A" through "G" (subways and buses), and the street map on page 44.

NAME	ADDRESS	PHONE	TYPE OF CUISINE
Adam's Rib	23 East 74 St.	535-2112	Steaks
Akita	12 East 44 St.	697-0342	Japanese
American Charcuterie	51 West 52 St.	751-5152	Deli.
Asian Pearl	972 2nd Ave.	421-2322	Chinese
Aurelio's	230 East 63 St.	832-1430	Steaks
Beefsteak Charlie	12 East 49 St.	753-1700	Steaks
Brazilian Coffee Restrnt.	45 West 46 St.	757-9352	Brazil.-Port
Cafe de la Paix	50 Central Pk. South	755-5800	French
Cafe des Artistes	1 West 67 St.	877-3500	French
Casa Bella	127 Mulberry St.	431-4080	Sicilian
Casa Brasil	406 East 85 St.	288-5284	Cont.-Braz.
Castilian	303 East 56 St.	688-6435	Spanish
Cheese Cellar	125 East 54 St.	758-6565	Fondues
City Luck	127 East 54 St.	832-2350	Cantonese
Da Silvano	260 Av. of the Amer.	982-0090	Italian
Dino & Henry's	132 West 32 St.	695-7995	Italian
DiPinto di Blu	54 West 45 St.	840-1284	Italian
Eleanora Ristorante	117 West 58 St.	765-1427	Italian
El Quijote	226 West 23 St.	929-1855	Spanish
Fisherman's Net, The	493 3rd Ave.	532-1683	Seafood
Foo Chow	1278 3rd Ave.	861-4350	Chinese
Giambone's	42 Mulberry St.	285-1277	Italian
Giovanni's Atrium	100 Washington St.	344-3777	Italian
Girafe	208 East 58 St.	752-3054	Italian
Harry's New York Bar	50 Central Pk. South	755-5800	Steaks
Haymarket (Statler)	7th Av. & 33 St.	736-5000	Amer.-Con
Holbrook's	1313 3rd Ave.	734-2050	American
Il Nido	251 East 53 St.	753-8450	Italian
Il Rigoletto	232 East 53 St.	759-9384	Italian
Jimmy La Grange	120 East 39 St.	686-4666	Continenta
Jimmy Weston's	131 East 54 St.	838-8384	American
Joe Burns'	903 1st Ave.	759-6696	American
K.C. Place	807 9th Ave.	246-4258	Seafood
Knickers	928 2nd Ave.	223-8821	Fr.-Amer.
La Chansonette	890 2nd Ave.	752-7320	French
La Fenice	242 East 58 St.	759-4660	Italian
La Strada East	274 3rd Ave.	473-3760	Italian
La Tulipe	104 West 13 St.	691-8860	French
La Toja	519 2nd Ave.	889-1909	Spanish
Laurent	111 East 56 St.	753-2729	French
Le Bistro	827 3rd Ave.	759-5933	French

Le Perigord	405 East 52 St.	755-6244	French
Le Plaisir	969 Lexington Ave.	734-9430	French
Le Steak	1089 2nd Ave.	421-9072	French
Lindy's	1256 Ave. of Amer.	586-8986	American
Little Club	945 2nd Ave.	832-2926	French
Louise, Junior	317 East 53 St.	355-9172	Ital.-Fr.
Maestro Cafe	58 West 65 St.	787-5990	American
Mamies	35 West 8 St.	673-8188	Waffles
McCarthy's	839 2nd Ave.	687-6131	Steaks
Mitsukoshi	465 Park Ave.	935-6444	Japanese
Mona Lisa	936 2nd Ave.	421-4497	Italian
Monsignore II	61 East 55 St.	355-2070	Italian
Mont D'Or	244 East 46 St.	697-5668	Fr.-Ital.
Mormando	541 Lexington Ave.	935-9570	Ital.-Cont.
Mrs. J's Sacred Cow	228 West 72 St.	873-4067	Continental
Nadia's Restaurant	994 2nd Ave.	888-6300	Italian
Nanni's	146 East 46 St.	697-4161	Italian
Nirvana	30 Central Pk. South	752-0270	India-Pak.
Old Homestead	56 9th Ave.	242-9040	American
Ole	434 2nd Ave.	725-1953	Spanish
Orchidia	145 2nd Ave.	473-8784	Ital.-Ukrain.
Orsini's	41 West 56 St.	757-1698	Italian
Peacock Alley	301 Park Ave.	355-3000	Continental
Peng's	219 East 44 St.	682-8050	Chinese
Per Bacco	140 East 27 St.	532-8699	Italian
Pete's Tavern	129 East 18 St.	473-7676	Ital.-Cont.
Rendezvous	21 East 52 St.	753-5970	French
Slate Steak House	852 10th Ave.	581-6340	Steaks
Spanish Taverna	203 West 38 St.	221-6458	Spanish
Thirty-seventh St. Hideaway	32 West 37 St.	947-8940	Ital.-Amer.
Tino's	235 East 58 St.	751-0311	Italian
Tom's Shangri-La	237 Madison Ave.	683-0996	Chinese
Torremolinos	230 East 51 St.	755-1862	Spanish
Toscana	246 East 54 St.	371-8144	Italian
Tuesday's	190 3rd Ave.	533-7900	American
Wellington Grill	65 East 56 St.	888-0830	English

GREENWICH VILLAGE, EAST VILLAGE and CHELSEA

Scale
0 ¼ Miles

The West Side Highway (an elevated, limited-access roadway) has been closed to all traffic for an indefinite period, pending completion of plans to reconstruct and reroute the highway. West Street and Twelfth Ave. can both be used for through traffic.

EAST RIVER

HUDSON RIVER

JACOB RIIS HOUSES

PETER COOPER VILLAGE

STUYVESANT TOWN

UNION SQUARE PK.

WASHINGTON SQ. PARK

TOMPKINS SQ. PK.

GREENWICH VILLAGE

EAST VILLAGE

CHELSEA

WEST SIDE HIGHWAY

FRANKLIN D. ROOSEVELT

36

Index to Greenwich Village Streets

LOWER MANHATTAN
CHINATOWN, SOHO
and
FINANCIAL DISTRICT

0   Scale in feet   500   1000

Lower Manhattan Streets

FINDING YOUR WAY AROUND NEW YORK

Remember that Manhattan Island, of which Midtown is the central portion, is long and thin — about two and one-half miles wide by more than twelve long. Central Park, aptly named, lies nearly at the geographical center. To the west is the Hudson River, and on the east is East River; New York Harbor is in the south. To the north is the Bronx and the mainland of New York State.

Most streets in the city are laid out on a rectangular grid modal. But this grid system is weak or does not exist at all in most parts of lower Manhattan, including Greenwich Village, and most of the island south of Canal Street.

Furthermore, Broadway cuts across the grid diagonally. There are twenty north-south blocks to the mile, but only seven east-west.

Some avenues are numbered, starting at 1 in the east, going up to 12 in the west. But Park Avenue South (Park Avenue south of 32 St.) was formerly 4th Av., and Avenue of the Americas was 6th Ave. Also, 8th Ave., where it borders Central Park on the west is called Central Park West. Similarly, 59th St. becomes Central Park South where it borders the park.

Beware of the term "downtown." It usually means Lower Manhattan south of Canal Street. And when New Yorkers say "out on the island," they usually do not mean Queens and Brooklyn, even though these two boroughs are on Long Island. They are referring to portions of Long Island outside New York City.

FINDING STREET NUMBERS

(For Finding Avenue numbers, see below this section)

In Midtown, the streets are numbered east and west from 5th Avenue. The diagram below shows how the street address numbers are divided between avenues, beginning at 5th Ave. Note that west of 5th Ave., street addresses are spaced 100 between each avenue. But east of 5th Ave., only 50 numbers separate each block until 3rd Ave. is reached.

Because Central Park occupies three east-west blocks, the numbering begins at Central Park West (8th Ave.) Street addresses with odd numbers are always found on the north side of the street; even numbers are on the south side.

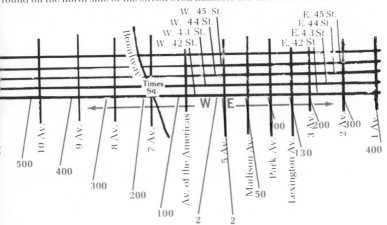

Numbering Between Avenues

Continued on next page

FINDING ADDRESSES ALONG AVENUES

Because all the avenues begin at different points, the numbers do not correspond. For example, at 43rd St. and 7th Ave., the 7th Ave. numbers are 1491 to 1502, but on Ave. of the Americas, the addresses are 1111 to 1120, and on 5th Ave. the addresses at 43rd St. are 500 to 520.

There is a system, however, that does permit one to find out where, to within a block or so, an avenue address can be found (midtown Manhattan only).

Cancel out the last figure of the house number, and then divide by 2. After this, add or subtract the key number given below:

Avenues A, B, C, D . . . . Add 3
First Avenue . . . . Add 3
Second Avenue . . . . Add 3
Third Avenue . . . . Add 10
Fourth Avenue . . . . Add 8
Fifth Avenue
    63 to 108 . . . . Add 11
    109 to 200 . . . . Add 13
    202 to 500 . . . . Add 17
    510 to 770 . . . . Add 19
    776 to 1283 . . . . Subtract 18
    1310 to 1494 . . . . For 1310,
subtract 20, and for every additional
20 street numbers increase deduction
by 1 e.g. 1330 = 22, etc.
Seventh Avenue
    1 to 1800 . . . . Add 12
    1800 and above . . . . Add 20
Eighth Avenue . . . . Add 9
Ninth Avenue . . . . Add 13
Tenth Avenue . . . . Add 14
Eleventh Avenue . . . . Add 15
Amsterdam Avenue . . . . Add 59
Audubon Avenue . . . . Add 165

Avenue of the Americas
    (Sixth Avenue) . . . . Subtract 12
Broadway
    Anything below 754 is south
    of 8th St., hence a named
    street.
    756 to 846 . . . . Subtract 29
    847 to 953 . . . . Subtract 25
    Above 953 . . . . Subtract 31
Central Park West
    Cancel last figure and add 60
Columbus Avenue . . . . Add 59 or 60
Convent Avenue . . . . Add 127
Fort Washington . . . . Add 158
Lenox Avenue . . . . Add 110
Lexington Avenue . . . .∴ Add 22
Madison Avenue . . . . Add 27
Manhattan Avenue . . . . Add 100
Park Avenue . . . . Add 34
Park Avenue South . . . . Add 8
Riverside Drive
    Cancel last figure and add 72
    up to 567. Beyond 568, add 78.
St. Nicholas Avenue . . . . . . Add 110

West End Avenue . . . . Add 59

For a comprehensive listing of all streets and house numbers, consult Geographia's *Complete Street Guide to New York.*

DRIVING IN NEW YORK CITY

The best advice is: DON'T.

Driving a car in Manhattan should be avoided if at all possible. But if you must drive, try to pick non-rush hours. The rush is from 7 a.m. to 9 a.m. and between 4:30 and 6:30 p.m. The density of traffic is perhaps the highest in the country, and in early Spring the streets are apt to be in a state of disrepair, due to the severity of winter.

Be alert and use a street map and index for getting about. Do not depend upon native informants. Their city is so big that few people are sufficiently familiar to be able to give viable directions to a stranger. However, to some extent you can rely upon taxi drivers, traffic police, and bus drivers.

Crosstown traffic usually moves best along 14th, 23rd, 34th, 42nd and 57th streets. No left turns, and no stopping or standing are permitted on these streets.

The West Side Highway is closed for modernization and rebuilding south of 46th Street.

Parking is prohibited on most downtown streets. The no-parking zone extends from 23rd to 72nd streets, except where metered. Parking garages charge from about $3.75 to $5.00 per day. There are about 1,000 private garages in the city. Some hotels maintain free parking service for their patrons — but only some.

Driving Tip.   You will pay more for a garage than you will for a taxi.

Warning.   Cars parked illegally in mid-town are ticketed almost without fail — your chances of avoiding a heavy fine are slim. Your car may be towed away, too. If your car is towed away, it will be found under the West Side Highway, at 36th Street. Call **Towaways** 239-2541.

During rush hours, traffic averages about four miles per hour.

One-Way Streets.   These are numerous and clearly marked with black and white arrows. Odd-number streets are most always west-bound, and even-numbered streets are east-bound. The one-way street pattern is too complex to show on our maps for all of New York City, but the pattern of mid-town is shown on page **15.**

For traffic and transit conditions, call **999-1234.**

To report potholes, call **566-2018.** The Parking Violations Bureau number is 481-6360.

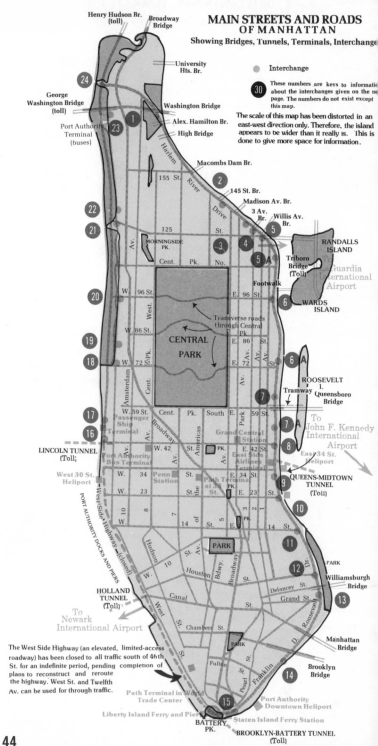

MAIN STREETS AND ROADS
OF MANHATTAN
Showing Bridges, Tunnels, Terminals, Interchange

● Interchange

30 These numbers are keys to information about the interchanges given on the next page. The numbers do not exist except this map.

The scale of this map has been distorted in an east-west direction only. Therefore, the island appears to be wider than it really is. This is done to give more space for information.

Henry Hudson Br. (toll)
Broadway Bridge
University Hts. Br.
George Washington Bridge (toll)
Port Authority Terminal (buses)
Washington Bridge
Alex. Hamilton Br.
High Bridge
Macombs Dam Br.
155 St.
145 St. Br.
Madison Av. Br.
3 Av. Br.
Willis Av. Br.
125 St.
Harlem River Drive
MORNINGSIDE PK.
Cent. Pk. No.
RANDALLS ISLAND
Triboro Bridge (Toll)
Guardia International Airport
Footwalk
WARDS ISLAND
W. 96 St.
E. 96 St.
Transverse roads through Central Pk
W. 86 St.
CENTRAL PARK
E. 86 St.
W. 72 St.
E. 72 St.
West Pk.
Amsterdam
Cent.
ROOSEVELT I.
Tramway
Queensboro Bridge
W. 59 St.
Cent. Pk. South
E. 59 St.
Passenger Ship Terminal
Broadway
Americas
Park Av.
To John F. Kennedy International Airport
LINCOLN TUNNEL (Toll)
Port Authority Bus Terminal
W. 42 St.
Grand Central Station
E. 42 St.
East Side Airlines Terminal
East 34 St. Heliport
West 30 St. Heliport
W. 34 St.
Penn Station
E. 34 St.
Path Terminal at 33 St.
QUEENS-MIDTOWN TUNNEL (Toll)
West Side Highway (closed)
W. 23 St.
E. 23 St.
W. 10
8
7
6th of the Av.
5
PK.
3 2 1
E. 14 St.
W. 14 St.
PARK
PORT AUTHORITY DOCKS AND PIERS
Hudson St.
10 St.
Av. of the
Bdwy.
Broadway
PARK
Williamsburgh Bridge
Houston St.
HOLLAND TUNNEL (Toll)
Canal St.
West St.
Delancey St.
Grand St.
Roosevelt Dr.
To Newark International Airport
Chambers St.
Manhattan Bridge
PARK
Fulton St.
Pearl St.
Franklin St.
Brooklyn Bridge
The West Side Highway (an elevated, limited-access roadway) has been closed to all traffic south of 46th St. for an indefinite period, pending completion of plans to reconstruct and reroute the highway. West St. and Twelfth Av. can be used for through traffic.
Path Terminal in World Trade Center
Port Authority Downtown Heliport
Liberty Island Ferry and Pier
Staten Island Ferry Station
BATTERY PK.
BROOKLYN-BATTERY TUNNEL (Toll)

44

KEYS TO THE INTERCHANGE NUMBERS SHOWN ON
THE MAP OF MAIN STREETS AND ROADS

1   Includes entrance to Harlem River Dr. from Edgecombe Av., and junction with Cross-Bronx Expwy. in both directions, and entrance to George Washington Bridge. all directions.

2   Ramp off to 143 St. and entrance to Harlem River Dr. from 5 Av.

3   Exits from Harlem River Drive to Park Av. and to 135 St.; on to Harlem River Drive from 139 St. in both directions.

4   Access to 3 Av. Bridge from Harlem River Drive and to 127 St. in both directions.

5   Interchange to Triboro Bridge. Queens routes. Bronx routes and the Willis Av. Bridge. to and from East River Drive and Harlem River Drive, all directions.

5A   116 St. interchange, downtown.

6   Entrance from 102 St., near the footbridge to Ward's Island, plus exit to 97 St., and 96 St. main interchange, both directions.

6A   79 St. and 73 St. interchange. Also exit to 82 St.

7   63 St. interchange in both directions.

7A   48 and 49 St. entrance to F.D.R. Drive uptown, off downtown side at 49 St. Cannot exit F.D.R. Drive north.

8   42 St. main interchange, both directions (but the downtown entrance to F.D.R. Drive is at 40 St.).

9   34 St. main interchange, both directions.

10   23 St. main interchange; ramp to F.D.R. Drive downtown is at 20 St.

11   14 St. main interchange in both directions.

12   Williamsburgh Bridge interchange. by way of Delancey St. only.

13   Grand St., both directions. There is no access to Manhattan Bridge from F.D.R. Drive.

14   Brooklyn Bridge—City Hall—Civic Center.

15   Brooklyn-Battery Tunnel.

16   Interchange closed; Lincoln Tunnel access is by way of 42 St., Dyer Av. and 41 St.

17   West Side Highway interchange for Henry Hudson Parkway; Downtown closed.

18   Entrance to Henry Hudson Parkway and Riverside Drive.

19   79 St. interchange in all directions.

20   96 St. interchange; best for crossing Central Park.

21   Interchange to Riverside Drive and 125 St.

22   145 St. interchange.

23   George Washington Bridge. local streets and Cross-Bronx Expwy.

24   Dyckman St.—Riverside Drive, direct access to Harlem River Drive.

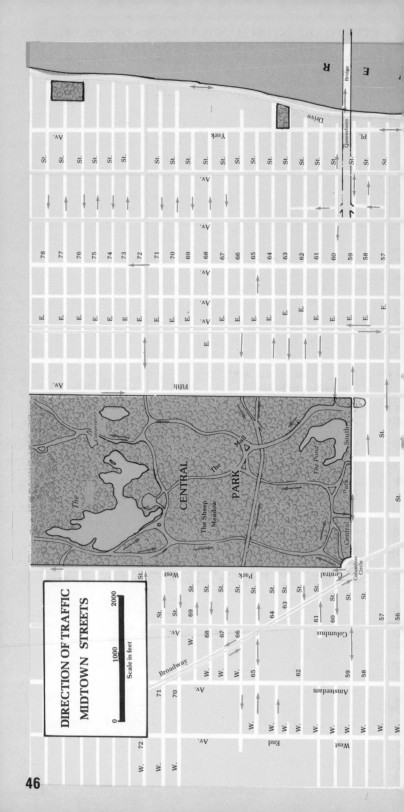

**DIRECTION OF TRAFFIC
MIDTOWN STREETS**

Scale in feet

0   1000   2000

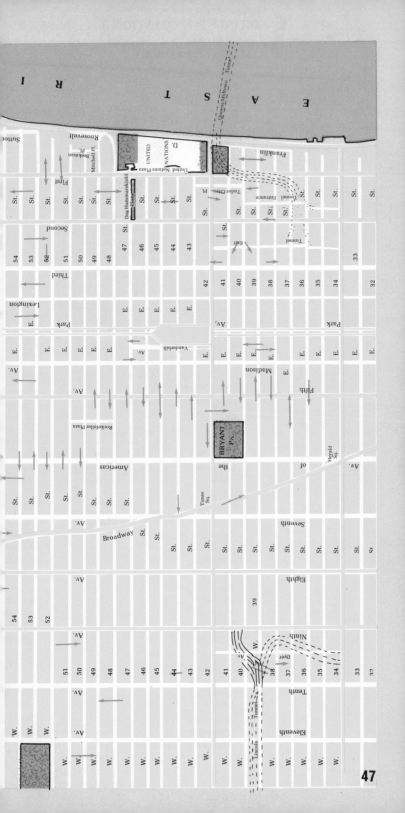

47

AIRLINES INFORMATION

DOMESTIC AIRLINES

New York Helicopter Svce.	895-1695
Air New England	
Toll Free	800 225-3640
Air Florida Inc	265-6140
Alaska Airlines Inc	800-426-0333
American Airlines	661-4242
Commuter Airlines	
Toll Free	800 252-1490
Delta Air Lines Inc	239-0700
Eastern Airlines	986-5000
Hawaiian Airlines	355-4843
National Airlines	697-9000
Northwest	564-2300
Ozark Air Lines	586-3612
Piedmont Airlines	489-1460
Republic Airlines	581-8851
TWA	290-2121
USAir	736-3200
United Airlines	867-3000

INTERNATIONAL AIRLINES

Aer Lingus-Irish	557-1110	Ethiopian Airlines	867-0099
Aerocondor The Airline		Finnair	889-7070
of Colombia	697-9303	Iberia Air Lines	
Aeroflot Soviet	661-4050	of Spain	793-3300
Aerolineas Argentinas	974-3300	Icelandic Airlines-	
Aeromexico	391-2900	Loftleidir	757-8585
Air Afrique	247-0100	Japan Air Lines	759-9100
Air Canada	869-1900	KLM Royal Dutch	
Air France	247-0100	Airlines	759-3600
Air-India	751-6200	Korean Air Lines	244-8330
Air Jamaica	421-9750	Kuwait Airways	581-9412
Air New Zealand Ltd	(914) 661-7444	Laker Airways Ltd	459-609.
Air Panama		Northwest Orient	563-7200
Internacional	246-4060	Olympic Airways	838-3600
Alitalia Airlines	582-8900	Pan Am	973-4000
American Airlines	661-4242	Qantas Airways	764-020
Arab Airlines	581-5600	Royal Air Maroc	974-379
Austrian Airlines	896-8623	Sabena Belgian	
BWIA	397-8800	World Airlines	961-620
Braniff International	687-8200	Scandinavian	657-770
British Airways	687-1600	Singapore Airlines	949-909
China Airlines	581-6500	Swissair	995-840
Costa Rica Airlines	245-6370	TAP The Airline	
Czechoslavak		of Portugal	944-210
Airlines—CSA	682-5833	Trans America	
Delta Air Lines	239-0700	Airlines	563-772
Dominicana Airlines	582-5616	Trans World	
Eastern Airlines	661-3500	Airlines Inc	290-212
Egyptair	581-5600	Varig Brazilian	682-310
El Al Israel	486-2600	World Airways Inc. Inc	267-711

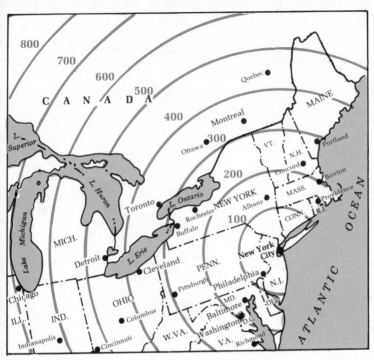

Air Distances From New York City

U.S. Cities		World Cities	
Albuquerque	1,815	Athens	4,938
Atlanta	748	Aukland (N.Z.)	10,194
Birmingham	864	Accra (Ghana)	5,126
Boston	188	Bangkok (Thailand)	8,669
Buffalo	292	Berlin	3,965
Charleston, S.C.	641	Bombay	7,811
Charlotte	533	Buenos Aires	5,602
Chicago	713	Cairo	5,602
Cincinnati	570	Calcutta	7,918
Cleveland	405	Cape Town	7,764
Dallas	1,374	Caracas	2,132
Denver	1,631	Frankfurt	4,028
Des Moines	1,022	Hong Kong	8,054
Detroit	482	Istanbul	4,975
El Paso	1,905	Jerusalem	5,344
Fargo	1,210	Keflavik (Iceland)	2,597
Honolulu	4,964	Kerachi (Pakistan)	7,277
Houston	1,420	Kinshasa (Zaire)	6,348
Indianapolis	646	Lima	3,635
Jacksonville	838	Lisbon	3,364
Kansas City, Mo.	1,097	London	3,458
Knoxville	632	Madrid	3,596
Los Angeles	2,451	Manila	8,498
Louisville	652	Melbourne	10,352
Memphis	957	Mexico City	2,094
Miami	1,092	Montreal	320
Minneapolis	1,018	Moscow	4,665
Nashville	761	Nairobi (Kenya)	7,365
New Orleans	1,171	New Delhi	7,319
Omaha	1,144	Oslo (Norway)	3,686
Philadelphia	83	Paris	3,624
Phoenix	2,145	Peking	6,867
Pittsburgh	317	Rabat (Morocco)	3,636
Portland, Oreg.	2,445	Rio de Janeiro	4,817
Raleigh	426	Rome	4,281
St. Louis	875	Santiago (Chile)	5,106
Salt Lake City	1,972	Shanghai	7,371
San Antonio	1,584	Shannon (Ireland)	3,086
San Francisco	2,571	Singapore	9,539
Seattle	2,408	Stockholm	3,924
Spokane	2,179	Sydney	9,933
Tulsa	1,231	Tehran	6,141
Washington, D.C.	205	Tokyo	6,740
Wichita	1,266	Vienna	4,233

KENNEDY AIRPORT

0   1

Scale in miles

JFK EXPRESS.

The New York City Transit Authority operates an express service between 57th Street and Kennedy Airport by way of the Independent Subway division tracks. The route is shown on PG.55 The fare is $4.00 Passengers leave the train at Howard Beach station and board buses which complete the trip. Total time is about one hour.

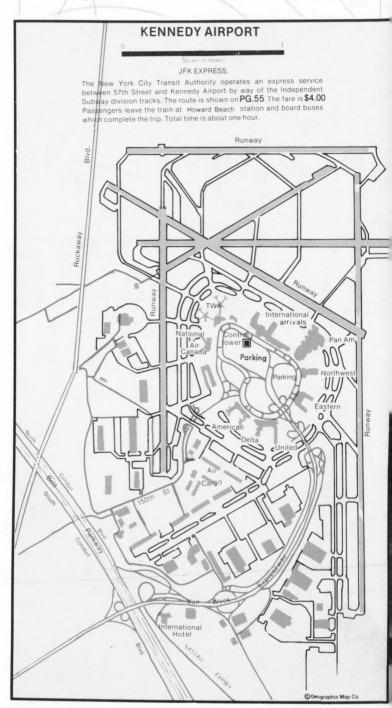

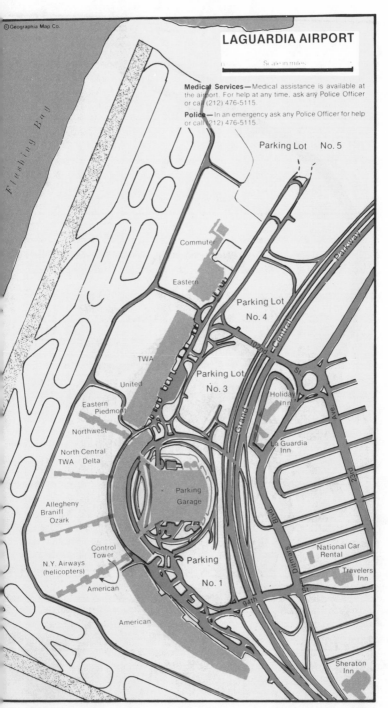

LAGUARDIA AIRPORT

Scale in miles

Medical Services—Medical assistance is available at the airport. For help at any time, ask any Police Officer or call (212) 476-5115.

Police—In an emergency ask any Police Officer for help or call (212) 476-5115.

Parking Lot No. 5

Flushing Bay

Commuter

Eastern

Parking Lot No. 4

TWA

United

Eastern
Piedmont

Northwest

North Central
TWA   Delta

Allegheny
Braniff
Ozark

Control
Tower

N.Y. Airways
(helicopters)

American

American

Parking Lot No. 3

Parking Garage

Parking No. 1

Grand

Central

102nd

St.

Parkway

Holiday Inn

La Guardia Inn

23rd Ave.

Ditmars Blvd.

94th St.

National Car Rental

Travelers Inn

Sheraton Inn

© Geographia Map Co.

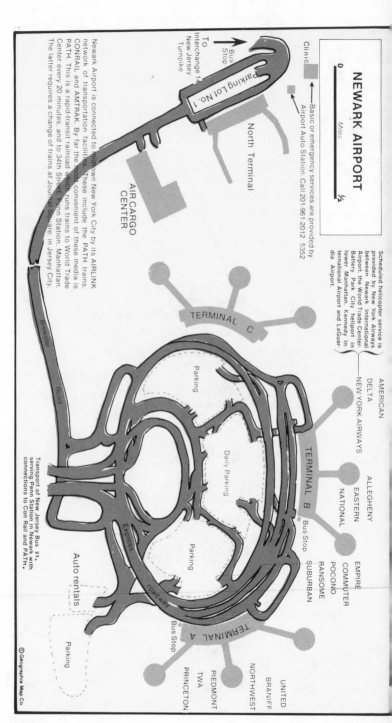

NEWARK AIRPORT

Miles
0   ¼

Scheduled helicopter service is provided by New York Airways between Newark International Airport, the World Trade Center, the Wall Street, Battery Park City heliport in lower Manhattan, Kennedy International Airport and LaGuardia Airport.

Basic or emergency services are provided by Airport Auto Station. Call 201-961-2012 5352

Clinic

Parking Lot No. 1

Bus Stop

To Interchange 14, New Jersey Turnpike

North Terminal

AIR CARGO CENTER

Brewster Road

TERMINAL C

AMERICAN
DELTA
NEW YORK AIRWAYS

Parking

Daily Parking

Parking

TERMINAL B

ALLEGHENY
EASTERN
NATIONAL

EMPIRE
COMMUTER
POCONO
RANSOME
SUBURBAN

Bus Stop

Express Roadway

TERMINAL A

Bus Stop

Auto rentals

Parking

UNITED
BRANIFF

NORTHWEST

TWA
PIEDMONT
PRINCETON

Newark Airport is connected to midtown New York City by its AIRLINK network of transportation facilities. These include the PATH trains, CONRAIL and AMTRAK. By far the most convenient of these media is PATH. This is a rapid-transit railroad which runs trains to World Trade Center every 20 minutes, and to 34th Street, Penn Station, Manhattan. The latter requires a change of trains at Journal Square, in Jersey City.

Transport of New Jersey Bus 21, serving Penn Station in Newark with connections to Con Rail and PATH.

© Geographia Map Co.

52

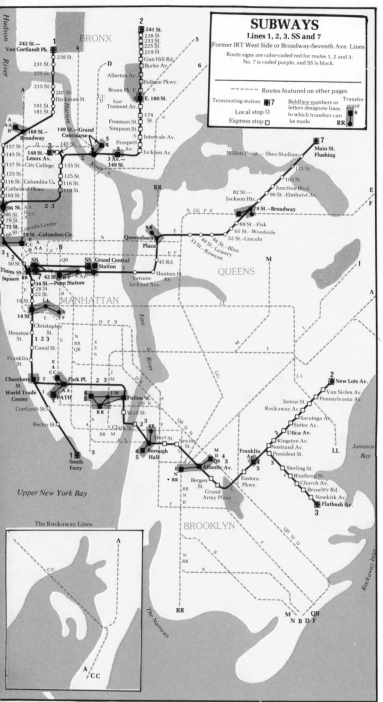

SUBWAYS
Lines 1, 2, 3, SS and 7
Former IRT West Side or Broadway-Seventh Ave. Lines

Route signs are color-coded red for routes 1, 2 and 3;
No. 7 is coded purple, and SS is black.

- - - - - Routes featured on other pages

Terminating station ■7   Boldface numbers or
Local stop ○   letters designate lines
Express stop □   to which transfers can
                          be made.

Transfer point ●6
RR ●

Hudson River

BRONX

242 St.— Van Cortlandt Pk. 1
238 St.
231 St.
225 St.
215 St.
207 St.
191 St.
181 St.
168 St.— Broadway
157 St.
145 St.
137 St.—City College
125 St.
116 St.—Columbia U.
Cathedral Pkwy.
103 St.
96 St.
86 St.
79 St.
72 St.
66 St.—Lincoln Center
59 St.—Columbus Cir.
50 St.
Times Square
42 St.
34 St.—Penn Station
28 St.
23 St.
18 St.
14 St.
Christopher St.
Houston St.
Canal St.
Franklin St.
Chambers St.
World Trade Center
Cortlandt St.
Rector St.
South Ferry

241 St. 2
238 St.
233 St.
225 St.
219 St.
Gun Hill Rd.
Burke Av.
Allerton Av.
Bronx Pk. E.
Pelham Pkwy.
E. 180 St.
East Tremont Av.
174 St.
Freeman St.
Simpson St.
Intervale Av.
Prospect Av.
Jackson Av.

Dyckman St.
Harlem River
Grand Concourse
145 St.
148 St.— Lenox Av.
135 St.
125 St.
116 St.
110 St.
3 Av.— 149 St.
149 St.— Grand Concourse

MANHATTAN

Park Pl. 2 3
Fulton St.
Wall St.
Clark St.
Borough Hall
Nevins St.
Hoyt St.
Atlantic Av.
Bergen St.
Grand Army Plaza

Willets Point— Shea Stadium
Main St. Flushing 7
111 St.
103 St.
Junction Blvd.
90 St.—Elmhurst Av.
82 St.— Jackson Hts.
74 St.—Broadway
69 St.—Fisk
61 St.—Woodside
52 St.—Lincoln
46 St.—Bliss
40 St.—Lowery
33 St.—Rawson
Queensboro Plaza
45 Rd.
Hunters Pt.
Vernon— Jackson Avs.
Grand Central Station

QUEENS

QB

New Lots Av. 2
Van Siclen Av.
Pennsylvania Av.
Junius St.
Rockaway Av.
Saratoga Av.
Sutter Av.
Utica Av.
Kingston Av.
Nostrand Av.
President St.
Franklin Av.
Sterling St.
Winthrop St.
Church Av.
Beverley Rd.
Newkirk Av.
Flatbush Av. 3

Eastern Pkwy.

BROOKLYN

Jamaica Bay

Rockaway Inlet

Upper New York Bay

The Rockaway Lines

The Narrows

A

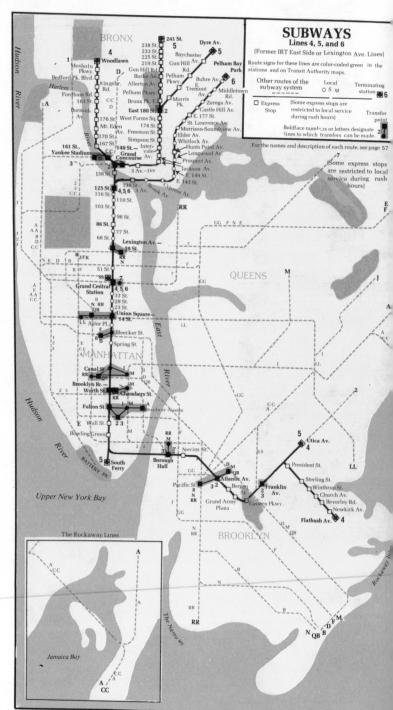

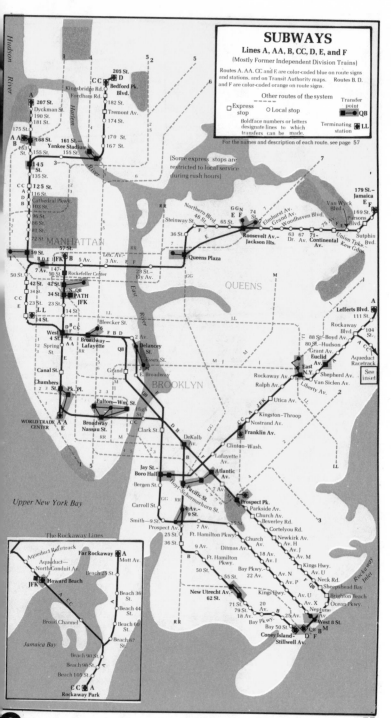

C

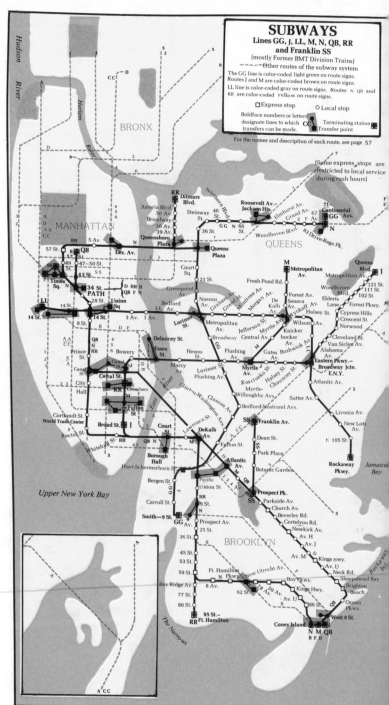

SUBWAYS
Lines GG, J, LL, M, N, QB, RR and Franklin SS
(mostly Former BMT Division Trains)
---⊖Other routes of the subway system

The GG line is color-coded light green on route signs.
Routes J and M are color-coded brown on route signs.
LL line is color-coded gray on route signs. Routes N QB and RR are color-coded yellow on route signs.

☐ Express stop   ○ Local stop

Boldface numbers or letters designate lines to which transfers can be made.   CC Terminating station   ▣ Transfer point

For the names and description of each route, see page 57

(Some express stops are restricted to local service during rush hours)

Hudson River

Harlem River

BRONX

MANHATTAN

QUEENS

BROOKLYN

Upper New York Bay

East River

The Narrows

Jamaica Bay

Ditmars Blvd.
Astoria Blvd.
30 Av.
Broadway
36 Av.
39 Av.
Steinway St.
46 St.
Roosevelt Av.–Jackson Hts.
Elmhurst Av.
Grand Av.
67 Av.
71–Continental Avs.
Queensboro Plaza
5 Av.
57 St.
QB St.
Lex. Av.
49 St.
47–50 Sts.
42 St.
Times Sq.
34 St. PATH
28 St.
Union Sq.
14 St.
8 St.
Prince St.
Canal St.
City Hall
Chambers
Fulton St.
Cortlandt St.
World Trade Center
Rector St.
Whitehall St.
Broad St.
Court St.
Borough Hall
Hoyt-Schermerhorn Sts.
Bergen St.
Carroll St.
Smith—9 St.
Prospect Av.
25 St.
36 St.
45 St.
53 St.
59 St.
Ft. Hamilton Pkwy.
8 Av.
Bay Ridge Av.
77 St.
86 St.
95 St.– Ft. Hamilton
New Utrecht Av.
62 St.
18 Av.
20 Av.
Bay Pkwy.
Kings Hwy.
Av. U
86 St.
West 8 St.
Coney Island
N M QB B F D
Ocean Pkwy.
Brighton Beach
Sheepshead Bay
Neck Rd.
Kings Hwy.
Av. U
Av. M
Av. J
Av. H
Newkirk Av.
Cortelyou Rd.
Beverley Rd.
Church Av.
Parkside Av.
Prospect Pk.
Botanic Garden
Park Place
Dean St.
Franklin Av.
Atlantic Av.
Pacific St.
Union St.
4 Av.
9 St.
Prospect Av.
DeKalb Av.
Atlantic Av.
Fulton St.
Lawrence St.
Court Sq.
21 St.
Greenpoint Av.
Nassau Av.
Graham Av.
Grand St.
Bedford Av.
Metropolitan Av.
Broadway
Lorimer St.
Flushing Av.
Marcy Av.
Hewes St.
Lorimer St.
Flushing Av.
Metropolitan Av.
Morgan Av.
Montrose Av.
De Kalb Av.
Jefferson St.
Central Av.
Myrtle Av.
Knickerbocker Av.
Gates Av.
Kosciusko St.
Myrtle Av.
Chauncey St.
Halsey St.
Bedford-Nostrand Avs.
Clinton-Washington Avs.
Classon Av.
Willoughby Avs.
Myrtle Av.
Fresh Pond Rd.
Metropolitan Av.
Forest Av.
Seneca Av.
Wyckoff Av.
Halsey St.
Wilson Av.
Bushwick Av.
Cleveland St.
Van Siclen Av.
Alabama Av.
Eastern Pkwy.– Broadway Jctn. E.N.Y.
Cypress Hills
Crescent St.
Norwood
Elderts Lane
Forest Pkwy.
Woodhaven Blvd.
102 St.
111 St.
121 St.
Metropolitan Av.
Queens Blvd.
Woodhaven Blvd.
63 Drive–Rego Pk.
Northern Blvd.
Sutter Av.
Atlantic Av.
Livonia Av.
New Lots Av.
E 105 St.
Rockaway Pkwy.
Queens Plaza
Delancey St.
Essex St.
Bowery
Canal St.
Metropolitan Av.

Rockaway Inlet

56

New York Subways Individual Route Descriptions

As the subway maps and the route descriptions below clearly indicate, the New York City subway route designations are being improved through the use of a color coding system.

The New York City Transit Authority is adopting this color-coding system in the belief that, with the use of color, the passenger will find it much easier to locate and follow desired routes.

We agree that it has many definite advantages for the subway rider. Therefore, we have attempted to provide a full description of the routes based on the new color coding.

Each of the subway system's major routes or route groups (which are essentially the former major divisions lines) will receive its own color. The color is used to enclose or surround the existing letters or numbers which designate individual lines or routes.

However, the change-over was not completed as of press time for this book. Upon completion, all route designations on the trains and on the platforms or stations will be coded with the appropriate route color.

The colors presently in use are orange, red, blue, dark green, light green, yellow, brown, black, purple and gray. The lines or routes of each color are described below.

BLUE LINES — Formerly the Independent System, Eighth Ave. Lines

KENNEDY AIRPORT EXPRESS

The New York City Transit Authority operates a daily passenger shuttle service, by subway, every 20 minutes from midtown to Kennedy Airport.*

The trains leave from 57 St. and Av. of the Americas, making the stops shown. The JFK Express terminates at Howard Beach station (see map C, page 24). From this station passengers are taken by bus to any air terminal. The bus is free; the subway fare $4.00 is collected on trains. Total time is about one hour. Note that the train stops only at the stations shown on this map. Passengers board trains at marked spots on each station platform.

It runs on the tracks of the **A** trains from W. 4 St. Manhattan to Howard Beach, where it is met by a shuttle bus (q.v. **A**).

Continued on next page

These were the former Independent System Routes that had been popularl
designated "Eighth Ave." and "Sixth Ave." trains, though none of the train
were exclusive to either avenues. (And Sixth Ave. is now Ave. of the Americas

A   A group of routes, popularly called the "The Eighth Ave. Trains." There a
three **As**; two of them known as **"Eighth Ave. Expresses,"** and the other is th
Rockaway Shuttle. Both expresses operate from 207 St., the Bronx, but on
goes to Far Rockaway and the other ends up at Lefferts Blvd. (both in Queens
They run all the time; are express in Manhattan, local in Queens, and expres
in Brooklyn during rush hours. The shuttle operates from Euclid Ave
Brooklyn to both Rockaway Park and Far Rockaway at night only.

AA   **Eighth Ave. Local,** operates between 168 St. and World Trade Center al
hours, except at night when the **A** is local in Manhattan.

CC   **Eighth Ave. Local.**   It is a rush-hour train, Manhattan only.

CC   **Shuttle,** from Broad Channel, Queens to Rockaway Park, Queens at all times
except rush hours and nights.

E   **Eighth Ave. Local.**   This train used to operate to Brooklyn, but is now
running at all times between World Trade Center and 179 St., Jamaica, Queens

LIGHT GREEN LINE

GG   **Brooklyn-Queens Crosstown (Local).** It has two divisions; one operate
between 71-Continental Aves.; in Queens and Smith-9 St., in Brooklyn; th
other is a nighttime train from Queens Plaza to Smith-9 St. Both are local a
all times.

YELLOW LINES —   Formerly BMT Trains

N   **Broadway Trains** — the heart of the former BMT system. There are four **Ns** –
two expresses, a local and a shuttle. The shuttle is nights only, betwee
36 St., Brooklyn and Coney Island. The Broadway Local runs between 71
Continental Aves., in Forest Hills, Queens, and Whitehall St., Manhattan
The two express run to Coney Island; one originates at 71-Continental Aves
Monday - Friday; the other is on a weekend and evening schedule, originatin
at 57 St., Manhattan.

QB   **Broadway Express,** a rush-hour train to Coney Island from 57 St., Manhattar
It is local in Brooklyn.

RR   **Broadway Local,** from Astoria, Queens to 95 St.—Ft. Hamilton, Brooklyr
at all times, always local.

RR   **Nassau St. Local,** from Chambers St., Manhattan to 95 St.—Ft. Hamilton
rush hours, local all the time.

Continued on next page

THE RED ROUTES — Formerly known as the IRT West Side or Seventh Ave. Lines

ORANGE LINES — Formerly Independent Sixth Ave. Lines

Broadway Local.   There are two of these; one operates between Van Cortlandt Pk. and South Ferry all the time; the other runs only between 137 St. and South Ferry Monday thru Friday, 8:00 A.M. — 5:30 P.M.

Seventh Ave. Express.   There are two routes, but the other one is a **No. 3** train (q.v.). **No. 2** operates between 241 St., in the Bronx and New Lots Ave., Brooklyn. It runs all the time; is express in Manhattan, local in Brooklyn.

Seventh Ave. Express.   Between 148 St.—Lenox Ave. (Harlem) and Flatbush Ave., Brooklyn. It runs all the time except nights; express in Manhattan and local in Brooklyn. At night, **No. 3** operates as a shuttle between 148 St. and a connection with the **No. 2** at 135 St.

GREEN ROUTES — Formerly the IRT East Side Lines

The Lexington Ave. Express.   There are four of them, all operating along the Woodlawn-Jerome Ave. (Bronx) tracks. Two of them go to Flatbush Ave., Brooklyn (one is a local in Brooklyn, but skips Hoyt St.; both are local in the Bronx but express in Manhattan). One **No. 4** operates to Atlantic Ave., Brooklyn, skips Hoyt St., but is local; the other goes to Utica Ave., Brooklyn, and is express in Manhattan and Brooklyn.

Lexington Ave. Express.   There are two **No. 5**s, and a third one that acts as a shuttle between Dyre Ave. and E. 180 St., in the Bronx at night. The two **No. 5**s operate from Dyre Ave., one goes only to Bowling Green, Manhattan; the other is a rush-hour train, express in Man. and Brklyn., goes to Utica Ave. In the Bronx, it makes all stops.

Lexington Ave. trains. . Three routes — two local and one express. One local and one express start at Pelham Bay Pk., in the Bronx, but all three routes terminate at Brooklyn Bridge. One local route operates from 177 St., Bronx, Monday thru Friday, and is express to Manhattan in the morning and from Manhattan in the evening.

PURPLE ROUTE — Main Street Flushing Line

Flushing Train.   Both express and local routes to Main St., Flushing Queens In Manhattan it runs under 42 St.

ORANGE LINES — Formerly Independent Sixth Ave. Lines

B   It is a group of routes (q.v. below) popularly called the **"Sixth Ave. Trains.**
This one has four versions — two as shuttles at night only (one in Manhatta
and one in Brooklyn); the **B Express** goes from 168 St., Manhattan to Cone
Island during rush hours; the B Local operates from 57 St., Manhattan t
Coney Island, except at night, when the shuttles are running.

D   **Sixth Ave. Express.**   There are two — one operates weekdays, 6:30 A.M. -
8:00 P.M., from 205 St., Bronx to Brighton Beach, Brooklyn; the other from
the same Bronx terminal to Coney Island at all other times. The Coney Islan
Train makes all stops in Brooklyn and the Bronx. The Brighton Beach Trai
is express in the Bronx and Brooklyn during rush hours.

F   **Sixth Ave. Local.**   Operates from 179 St., Jamaica, Queens to Coney Island
at all times; in Manhattan it is local except in rush hours (at which time
trains marked "Coney Island" operate express to Kings Highway, Brookly
in the morning and are local at night). In Queens, on week days. the F i
express between 179 St. and Queens Plaza. At other daytime hours, it i
express to Queens Plaza from 71—Continental Ave., but at night makes a
stops. In Brooklyn. the **F** is local except as noted above.

BROWN LINES — Formerly BMT Lines

J   **Nassau St. Local.**   Operates in Brooklyn and Queens, between Queens Blvd
and Broad St., Manhattan. During rush hours. it runs on a skip-stop schedul
in Queens, and also is express between Marcy Ave. and Myrtle Ave
Brooklyn.

M   **Nassau St. Local.**   There are two. One is a shuttle between Metropolita
Ave., Brooklyn and Myrtle Ave., Brooklyn, running evenings, nights an
weekends. local all the time; the other is a Coney Island train to Metropolita
Ave., Monday-Friday; local all the way and all the time.

Gray Line

LL   **14 St. — Canarsie Local,** operates between Eighth Ave., Manhattan, and
Rockaway Pkwy., Canarsie, Brooklyn; local all the time.

SPECIALS — BLACK LINES

S   **Times Square Shuttle.**   Operates all the time between Grand Central Station
and Times Square. There are no stations between the two terminals.

S   **Franklin Ave. Shuttle** (Brooklyn). It runs between Franklin Ave. and
Prospect Park, all the time, to make connections with **D, M, QB, and A.**

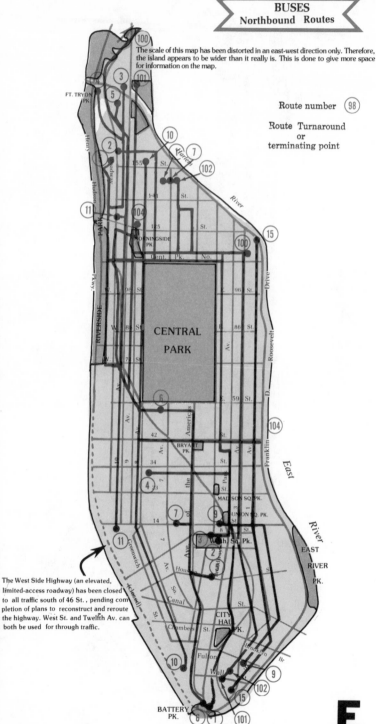

BUSES
Northbound Routes

The scale of this map has been distorted in an east-west direction only. Therefore, the island appears to be wider than it really is. This is done to give more space for information on the map.

Route number (98)

Route Turnaround
or
terminating point

CENTRAL PARK

FT. TRYON PK.

MORNINGSIDE PK.

RIVERSIDE PK.

BRYANT PK.

MADISON SQ. PK.

UNION SQ. PK.

Wash. Sq. Pk.

EAST RIVER PK.

CITY HALL PK.

BATTERY PK.

The West Side Highway (an elevated, limited-access roadway) has been closed to all traffic south of 46 St., pending completion of plans to reconstruct and reroute the highway. West St. and Twelfth Av. can both be used for through traffic.

E
61

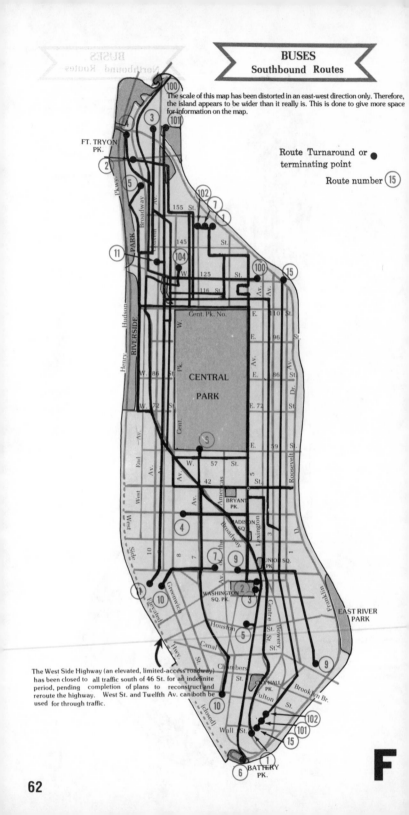

The scale of this map has been distorted in an east-west direction only. Therefore, the island appears to be wider than it really is. This is done to give more space for information on the map.

Route Turnaround or terminating point ●

Route number ⑮

FT. TRYON PK.

PARK

Broadway

155 St.

145 St.

Hudson

RIVERSIDE

Henry

W 125 St.

116 St.

Cent. Pk. No.

E. 110 St.

E. 96 St.

CENTRAL PARK

W. 86 St.

E. 86 St.

Pk.

Cent.

W 72 St.

E. 72 St.

Dr.

Av.

End

W. 57 St.

E. 59 St.

Roosevelt

West

Av.

Amsterdam

42 St.

BRYANT PK.

MADISON SQ.

Broadway

Lexington

West

10

8

7

UNION SQ.

WASHINGTON SQ. PK.

Greenwich

Centre St.

Bowery

Franklin

EAST RIVER PARK

Houston

Canal

Chambers St.

Hwy.

(closed)

CITY HALL PK.

Brooklyn Br.

Fulton St.

Wall St.

The West Side Highway (an elevated, limited-access roadway) has been closed to all traffic south of 46 St. for an indefinite period, pending completion of plans to reconstruct and reroute the highway. West St. and Twelfth Av. can both be used for through traffic.

BATTERY PK.

F

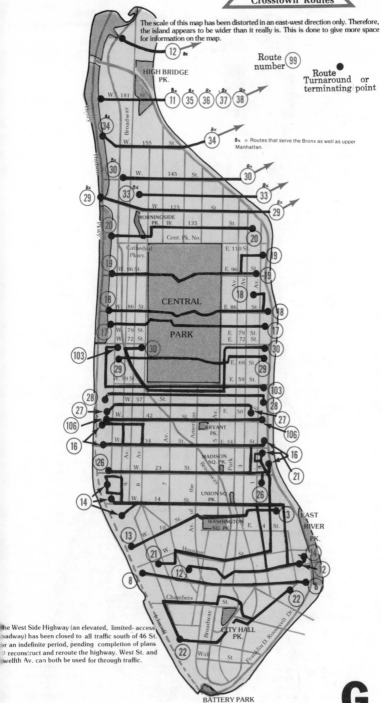

BUSES
Crosstown Routes

The scale of this map has been distorted in an east-west direction only. Therefore, the island appears to be wider than it really is. This is done to give more space for information on the map.

Route number ⑨⑨

● Route Turnaround or terminating point

𝐵ₓ = Routes that serve the Bronx as well as upper Manhattan.

HIGH BRIDGE PK.

CENTRAL PARK

MORNINGSIDE PK.

Cathedral Pkwy.

BRYANT PK.

MADISON SQ. PK.

UNION SQ. PK.

WASHINGTON SQ. PK.

EAST RIVER PK.

Chambers St.

CITY HALL PK.

Wall St.

Franklin D. Roosevelt Dr.

The West Side Highway (an elevated, limited-access roadway) has been closed to all traffic south of 46 St. for an indefinite period, pending completion of plans to reconstruct and reroute the highway. West St. and Twelfth Av. can both be used for through traffic.

BATTERY PARK

G
63

POINTS OF INTEREST
Manhattan

The scale of this map has been distorted in an east-west direction only. Therefore the island appears to be wider than it really is. This is done to give more space for information on the map.

1 Dyckman House
2 The Cloisters
3 George Washington Bridge
4 Morris-Jumel Mansion
5 Museum group and American Geographical Society
6 Hamilton Grange
7 General Grant National Mem.
8 Riverside Church
9 Cathedral Church of St. John the Divine
10 Central Park
11 Guggenheim Museum
12 American Museum of Natural History
13 Hayden Planetarium
14 New York Historical Society
15 The Mall
16 ZOO
17 R.C.A. Building
18 The Mill, Burlington House
19 Lincoln Center for the Performing Arts
20 The Coliseum
21 Rockefeller Center
22 Broadway theater district
23 Times Square
24 Radio City Music Hall
25 Madison Square Garden Center
26 Penn Station
27 Garment district
28 Macy's department store
29 Gimbel's department store
30 Kodak Gallery and photo information center
31 Greenwich Village
32 Holland Tunnel
33 John Street Church
34 Fire Department museum
35 Ellis Island Nat. Mon.
42 Statue of Liberty Nat. Mon.

36 Federal Reserve Bank
37 Woolworth Building
38 World Trade Center
39 St. Paul's Chapel
40 Trinity Church
41 American Stock Exchange
43 Old U.S. Customs building
44 Wall Street
45 Battery Park

Harlem

Columbia University
Museum of the City of New York
Jewish Museum
Cooper-Hewitt Museum
Gracie Mansion
Metropolitan Museum of Art
Cleopatra's Needle (obelisk)
Temple Emanu-El
Frick Collection (art)
Art Galleries
Whitney Museum of Art
Cable Tramway to Roosevelt Island 59
Park Ave. buildings 59
Citicorp Center
African-American Institute
United Nations
Museum of Modern Art
St. Patrick's Cathedral
Pan Am building
Grand Central Station and Visitors Bureau
Museum of Broadcasting
New York Public Library
Pierpont Morgan Library
Empire State building
Police Academy museum
Theodore Roosevelt Birthplace
St. Marks-in-the-Bowery
Old Merchant's House
Chinatown
Brooklyn Bridge
City Hall
South Street Seaport
Federal Hall (restoration)
New York Stock Exchange
Fraunces Tavern
Castle Clinton National Monument

The West Side Highway, an elevated, limited access roadway, has been closed to all traffic for an indefinite period, pending completion of plans to reconstruct and reroute the highway.

*Indicates points of interest described on pages **8-13**. Major Points of Interest in New York City: How to Get there and When to go

Number on map	Name	Address
* 61	African-American Institute, 833 United Nations Plaza	
* 5	American Geographical Society, Broadway at 155 St.	
* 12	American Museum of Natural History, Central Pk. West at 81 St.	
* 41	American Stock Exchange, 86 Trinity Pl.	
56	Art Galleries and Dealers, West Broadway (Lower Manhattan), and along Madison Ave. between 60 and 79 sts.	
* 45	Battery Park, southern tip of Manhattan (area called South Ferry)	
22	Broadway theater district, on both sides of Broadway, between 5th and 7th avenues, from Times Sq. north to 52 St.	
76	Brooklyn Bridge, East Side, Lower Manhattan, near City Hall	
* 82	Castle Clinton National Monument, Battery Park (q.v.)	
* 9	Cathedral Church of St. John the Divine (Episcopal) 1047 Amsterdam Av.	
* 10	Central Park, 59 to 110 sts., 5 Av. to Central Pk. W. (8 Av.)	
* 75	Chinatown, Lower Manhattan, between Bowery, Chatham Sq. and Canal St.	
60	Citicorp Center, Lexington Av. and 54 St.	
77	City Hall, Lower Manhattan between Park Row and Broadway	
53	Cleopatra's Needle (ancient Egyptian obelisk), Central Park	
2	Cloisters, The Fort Tryon Park, 190 St. and Ft. Washington Av.	
20	Coliseum, at Columbus Circle and 59 St. (8 Av.)	
* 47	Columbia University, Broadway at 116 St.	
50	Cooper-Hewitt Museum, 2 East 91 St.	
1	Dyckman House, 4881 Broadway	
35	Ellis Island, in New York Harbor	
70	Empire State Building, 350 5th Av.	
79	Federal Hall National Memorial, 28 Wall St.	
36	Federal Reserve Bank, 33 Liberty St.	
34	Fire Department Museum, 104 Duane St.	
81	Fraunces Tavern, 54 Pearl St.	
55	Frick Collection (art), 1 East 70 St.	
27	Garment district, between Ave. of the Americas and 7 Av., 34 to 40 sts.	
7	General Grant National Memorial, Riverside Dr. and 122 St.	
3	George Washington Bridge, 181 St. and Hudson River	
29	Gimbel's Department Store, 33 St. at Herald Square	
51	Gracie Mansion, Carl Schurz Pk., near East 89 St.	
31	Greenwich Village, 14 St. south to Houston St.	
6	Hamilton Grange, 287 Convent Av., near 141 St.	
46	Harlem, upper Manhattan, 110 St. to 155 St.	
13	Hayden Planetarium, 81 St. and Central Pk. W.	
32	Holland Tunnel, West end of Canal St., lower Manhattan	
33	John Street Church (United Methodist), 44 John St.	
49	Jewish Museum, 1109 5 Av., at 92 St.	
30	Kodak Gallery and Information Center, 1113 Ave. of the Americas	
19	Lincoln Center for the Performing Arts, Broadway at 64 St.	
28	Macy's Department Store, 34th St., Herald Square	
25	Madison Square Garden Center, between 7th and 8th Av., 31 St.	
15	The Mall, Central Park	

Continued on next page

† See also points of interests , Lower Manhattan

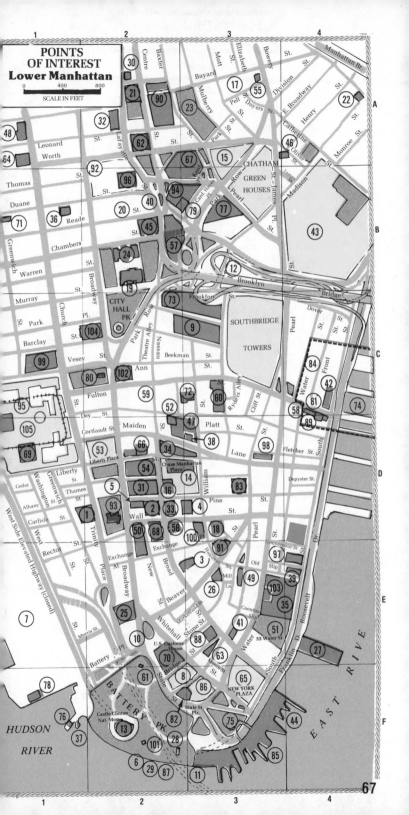

POINTS OF INTEREST
Lower Manhattan

SCALE IN FEET
0   400   800

HUDSON RIVER

EAST RIVER

BATTERY PK.

CITY HALL PK.

CHATHAM GREEN HOUSES

SOUTHBRIDGE TOWERS

Brooklyn Bridge

Manhattan Br.

Chase Manhattan Plaza

NEW YORK PLAZA

U.S. Customs House

Castle Clinton Nat. Mon.

West Side Elevated Highway (closed)

Franklin D. Roosevelt Dr.

POINTS OF INTEREST
LOWER MANHATTAN

Number on map	Name and Address	Map Key
1	American Stock Exchange, 86 Trinity Place	D-
2	Bankers Trust Building, 16 Wall St.	D-
3	Bank of America, 41 Broad St.	E-
4	Bank of Manhattan Tower, 40 Wall St.	D-
5	Bank of Tokyo Building (1895), 100 Broadway	D-
6	Battery Park and Promenade	F-
7	Battery Park City, on fill land from Pier A to Chambers St. (under construction)	E-
8	Battery Park Plaza	F-
9	Beekman Downtown Hospital, 170 William St.	C-
10	Bowling Green Park	E-
11	Brooklyn Battery Tunnel, Battery Pk. and S. Ferry	F-
12	Brooklyn Bridge, Park Row and Printing House Sq.	B-
13	Castle Clinton National Monument, Battery Park	F-
14	Chase Manhattan Plaza and No. 1, Liberty & Pine	D-
15	Chatham Towers	A-
16	Chemical Bank, New York Trust, 20 Pine St.	D-
17	Chinatown	A-
18	Citibank Building (1836), formerly Old Merchant's Exchange, 55 Wall St.	D-
19	City Hall and Park	B-
20	Civic Center Area	B-
21	Civil and Municipal Court, 111 Centre St.	A-
22	Clark, William (house), 1824, at 51 Market St.	A-
23	Columbus Park, Baxter and Worth sts.	A-
	Criminal Court Building, see Tombs, The	
24	Criminal Courthouse, Old (1872)	B-
25	Cunard Building, 25 Broadway	E-
26	Delmonico's (1891), 56 Beaver St.	E-
27	Downtown Heliport	E-
28	East Coast War Memorial, Battery Pk.	F-
29	Ellis Island National Monument, New York Harbor Ferry Slip at Promenade, Battery Park	F-
30	Engine Company No. 31, 87 Lafayette St.	A-
31	Equitable Life Ins. Bldg., 120 Broadway	D-
32	Family Court, 60 Lafayette St.	A-
33	Federal Hall National Memorial (1862), 28 Wall St. (includes museum)	D-
34	Federal Reserve Bank of New York, 33 Liberty	D-
	Fifty-one Market St., see Clark, William	
35	Fifty-Five Water St.	E-
36	Fire Department Museum, 104 Duane St.	B-
37	Fire Dept. Pier, at Pier A, West Side of Battery Park	F-
38	Firefighters Museum, Home Insurance Co., 59 Maiden Lane	D-
39	First Precinct Station House (police), 1909, at Old Slip and Water sts.	E-
40	Foley Square (courthouses)	B-
41	Fraunces Tavern (1927), 54 Pearl St.	E-
42	Fulton Fish Market, 94 South St.	C-
43	Governor Alfred E. Smith Houses	B-
44	Governor's Island Ferry slip	F-
45	Hall of Records, 31 Chambers St.	B-
46	Hebrew Burial Ground (old Jewish cemetery)	A-
47	Home Insurance Co. building, 60 John St.	C-
48	Department of Social Services	A-
49	India House (private club), 1851, No. 1 Hanover Square	E-
50	Irving Trust Co. building, 1 Wall St.	D-
51	Jeanette Park, Coenties Slip and Water St.	E-
52	John St. Methodist Church (1840), 44 John	D-
53	Liberty Plaza, formerly 165 Broadway	D-

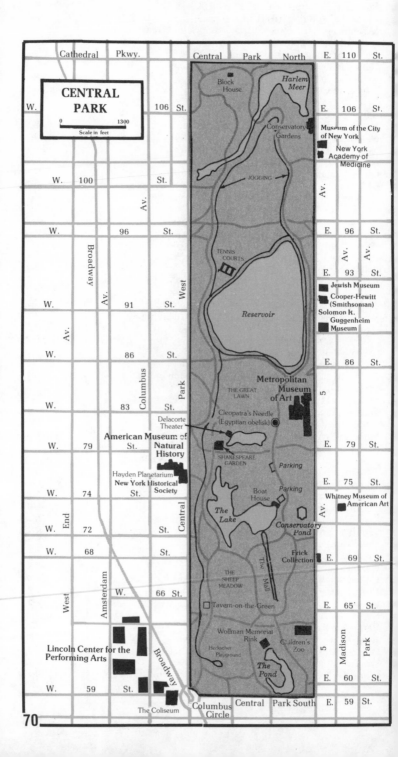

CENTRAL PARK

Scale in feet
0   1300

Cathedral Pkwy.

Central Park North

E. 110 St.

W. 106 St.

E. 106 St.

Block House

Harlem Meer

Conservatory Gardens

Museum of the City of New York

New York Academy of Medicine

W. 100 St.

JOGGING

W. 96 St.

E. 96 St.

Broadway

West Park

TENNIS COURTS

Av.

E. 93 St.

Jewish Museum

Cooper-Hewitt (Smithsonian)

W. 91 St.

Reservoir

Solomon K. Guggenheim Museum

Columbus Av.

W. 86 St.

E. 86 St.

THE GREAT LAWN

Metropolitan Museum of Art

W. 83 St.

Delacorte Theater

Cleopatra's Needle (Egyptian obelisk)

American Museum of Natural History

W. 79 St.

E. 79 St.

SHAKESPEARE GARDEN

Hayden Planetarium
New York Historical Society

Parking

Central Park West

W. 74 St.

E. 75 St.

Boat House

Parking

Whitney Museum of American Art

West End Av.

W. 72 St.

The Lake

Conservatory Pond

W. 68 St.

St.

Frick Collection

E. 69 St.

Amsterdam

THE SHEEP MEADOW

The Mall

W. 66 St.

E. 65 St.

Tavern-on-the-Green

Wollman Memorial Rink

5 Madison Park Av.

Lincoln Center for the Performing Arts

Heckscher Playground

Children's Zoo

W. 59 St.

Broadway

The Pond

E. 60 St.

The Coliseum

Columbus Circle

Central Park South

E. 59 St.

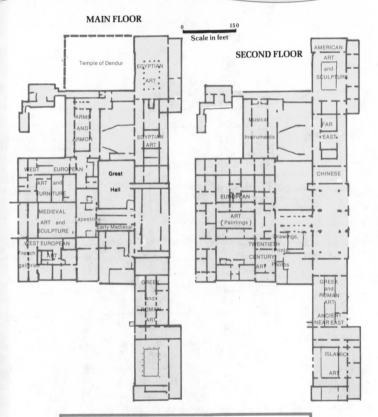

METROPOLITAN MUSEUM OF ART

MAIN FLOOR

Scale in feet
0   150

SECOND FLOOR

Temple of Dendur

EGYPTIAN ART

AMERICAN ART and SCULPTURE

Musical Instruments

FAR EAST

ARMS AND ARMOR

EGYPTIAN ART

CHINESE

WEST EUROPEAN ART and FURNITURE

Great Hall

MEDIEVAL ART and SCULPTURE

Tapestries

Early Medieval

EUROPEAN ART (Paintings)

WEST EUROPEAN French Art galleries

TWENTIETH CENTURY ART

Drawings, Prints

Photos

GREEK and ROMAN ART

GREEK and ROMAN ART

ANCIENT NEAR EAST

ISLAMIC ART

The Metropolitan Museum of Art was founded in 1870, and opened in 1872. The present main building dates from 1902, but is still unfinished. The museum contains 236 galleries, with over 5,000 European paintings and drawings, over 1,000,000 prints, 4,000 objects of medieval art, 3,000 American paintings and statues, and 4,000 musical instruments. Space limitations on this page prevent showing all the many departments and rooms. The two main floors we show contain on display at any one time about one-fourth of the museum's total collection.

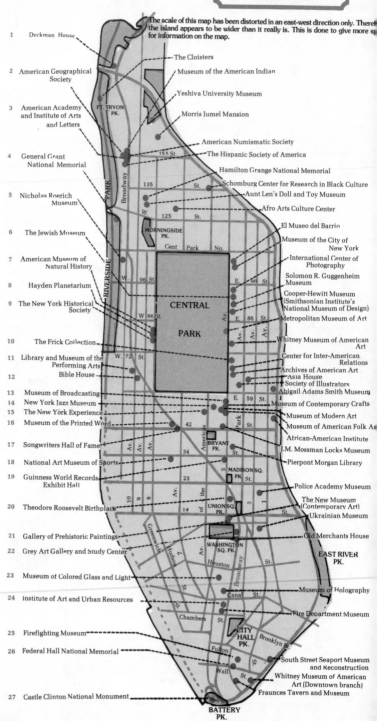

MUSEUMS

The scale of this map has been distorted in an east-west direction only. Therefore the island appears to be wider than it really is. This is done to give more space for information on the map.

1 Dyckman House

The Cloisters

2 American Geographical Society

Museum of the American Indian

Yeshiva University Museum

3 American Academy and Institute of Arts and Letters

Morris Jumel Mansion

American Numismatic Society

4 General Grant National Memorial

The Hispanic Society of America

Hamilton Grange National Memorial

Schomburg Center for Research in Black Culture

5 Nicholas Roerich Museum

Aunt Len's Doll and Toy Museum

Afro Arts Culture Center

El Museo del Barrio

6 The Jewish Museum

Museum of the City of New York

7 American Museum of Natural History

International Center of Photography

Solomon R. Guggenheim Museum

8 Hayden Planetarium

Cooper-Hewitt Museum (Smithsonian Institute's National Museum of Design)

9 The New York Historical Society

Metropolitan Museum of Art

10 The Frick Collection

Whitney Museum of American Art

11 Library and Museum of the Performing Arts

Center for Inter-American Relations

Archives of American Art

12 Bible House

Asia House

Society of Illustrators

13 Museum of Broadcasting

Abigail Adams Smith Museum

14 New York Jazz Museum

Museum of Contemporary Crafts

15 The New York Experience

Museum of Modern Art

16 Museum of the Printed Word

Museum of American Folk Art

African-American Institute

17 Songwriters Hall of Fame

J.M. Mossman Locks Museum

18 National Art Museum of Sports

Pierpont Morgan Library

19 Guinness World Records Exhibit Hall

Police Academy Museum

The New Museum (Contemporary Art)

20 Theodore Roosevelt Birthplace

Ukrainian Museum

21 Gallery of Prehistoric Paintings

Old Merchants House

22 Grey Art Gallery and Study Center

23 Museum of Colored Glass and Light

Museum of Holography

24 Institute of Art and Urban Resources

Fire Department Museum

25 Firefighting Museum

26 Federal Hall National Memorial

South Street Seaport Museum and Reconstruction

Whitney Museum of American Art (Downtown branch)

Fraunces Tavern and Museum

27 Castle Clinton National Monument

FT. TRYON PK.

155 St.

Broadway

135 St.

W. 125 St.

MORNINGSIDE PK.

Cent   Park   No.

CENTRAL PARK

W 96 St.

W 86 St.

W. 72 St.

E. 9th St.

E. 86 St.

RIVERSIDE

PARK

E. 59 St.

42

Americas

BRYANT PK.

34

Park

23

MADISON SQ. PK.

10 9 8

of the

14

UNION SQ. PK.

3 1

Greenwich

Hudson 7 Av.

WASHINGTON SQ. PK.

Houston   St.

Broadway

Canal St.

Chambers St.

CITY HALL PK.

Fulton St.

Brooklyn Br.

Wall St.

EAST RIVER PK.

BATTERY PK.

Number on map	Name	Address	Phone
49	Adams, Abigail Smith, Museum	421 East 61 St.	838-6878
53	African-American Institute	833 UN Plaza	949-5666
37	Afro Arts Culture Center	2191 Adam C. Powell, Jr. Blvd. (7 Av.)	831-3922
3	American Academy and Institute of Arts and Letters	Broadway & 156 St.	286-1480
46	American Art, Archives of	41 East 65 St.	826-5722
52	American Folk Art, Museum of	49 West 53 St.	LT 1-2474
2	American Geographical Society	Broadway & 156 St.	234-8100
29	American Indian, Museum of the	Broadway & 155 St.	283-2420
7	American Museum of Natural History	Cent. Pk. W. & 79 St.	873-4225
32	American Numismatic Society	Broadway & 155 St.	286-3030
24	Art and Urban Resources, Institute of (Clocktower Office)	108 Leonard St.	233-1096
47	Asia House Gallery	112 East 64 St.	751-4210
36	Aunt Len's Toy and Doll Museum	6 Hamilton Terrace	926-4172
38	Barrio, El Museo del	1230 5 Av.	831-7272
42	Bible House	1865 Broadway	581-7400
35	Black Culture, Schomburg Center for Research in	103 West 135 St.	862-4000
43	Broadcasting, Museum of	1 East 53 St.	752-7684
27	Castle Clinton National Monument	Battery Park	344-7220
28	Cloisters, The	Ft. Tryon Pk.	923-3700
23	Colored Glass and Light, Museum of	72 Wooster St.	226-7258
42	Cooper-Hewitt Museum (Smithsonian's National Museum of Design)	2 East 91 St.	860-6868
40	Crafts, Contemporary, Museum of	29 West 53 St.	397-0630
1	Dyckman House Museum	Broadway & 204 St.	WA 3-8008
	El Museo del Barrio. See Barrio		
6	Federal Hall National Memorial	26 Wall St.	264-8711
51	Fire Department Museum	104 Duane St.	RH 4-1000
25	Firefighting Museum	59 Maiden Lane	530-6800
54	Fraunces Tavern	54 Pearl St.	425-1776
40	Frick Collection, The	1 East 70 St.	288-0700
4	General Grant National Memorial	122 St. & Riverside Dr.	666-1640
2	Grey Art Gallery and Study Center	33 Washington Pl. New York University	598-7603
1	Guggenheim, Solomon R., Museum of Art	5 Av. at 89 St.	860-1300
9	Guiness World Record Exhibit Hall	2 Park Av.	532-7725
4	Hamilton Grange National Memorial	287 Convent Av.	283-5154

Continued on next page

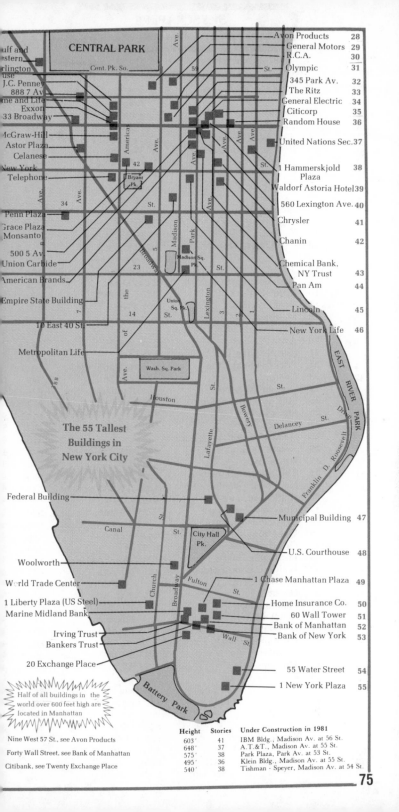

The 55 Tallest Buildings in New York City

CENTRAL PARK

Building	No.
Avon Products	28
General Motors	29
R.C.A.	30
Olympic	31
345 Park Av.	32
The Ritz	33
General Electric	34
Citicorp	35
Random House	36
United Nations Sec.	37
1 Hammerskjold Plaza	38
Waldorf Astoria Hotel	39
560 Lexington Ave.	40
Chrysler	41
Chanin	42
Chemical Bank, NY Trust	43
Pan Am	44
Lincoln	45
New York Life	46
Municipal Building	47
U.S. Courthouse	48
1 Chase Manhattan Plaza	49
Home Insurance Co.	50
60 Wall Tower	51
Bank of Manhattan	52
Bank of New York	53
55 Water Street	54
1 New York Plaza	55

Other labels:
Gulf and Western, Burlington House, J.C. Penney, 888 7 Ave., Time and Life, Exxon, 1133 Broadway, McGraw-Hill, Astor Plaza, Celanese, New York Telephone, Penn Plaza, Grace Plaza, Monsanto, 500 5 Av., Union Carbide, American Brands, Empire State Building, 10 East 40 St., Metropolitan Life, Federal Building, Woolworth, World Trade Center, 1 Liberty Plaza (US Steel), Marine Midland Bank, Irving Trust, Bankers Trust, 20 Exchange Place

Half of all buildings in the world over 600 feet high are located in Manhattan

Nine West 57 St., see Avon Products

Forty Wall Street, see Bank of Manhattan

Citibank, see Twenty Exchange Place

	Height	Stories	Under Construction in 1981
	603'	41	IBM Bldg., Madison Av. at 56 St.
	648'	37	A.T.&T., Madison Av. at 55 St.
	575'	38	Park Plaza, Park Av. at 53 St.
	495'	36	Klein Bldg., Madison Av. at 55 St.
	540'	38	Tishman - Speyer, Madison Av. at 54 St.

SKYSCRAPERS
The 55 Tallest Buildings in New York City

(For an alphabetical list, see next page)

Number on map	Rank in height	Name	Address	Height above street (in feet)	Stori
22	1	World Trade Center	Lower Manhattan (twin towers)	1,350	11
17	2	Empire State Building	350 5th Av.	1,250	10
41	3	Chrysler	405 Lexington Av.	1,046	7
51	4	Sixty Wall Tower	70 Pine St.	950	6
52	5	Bank of Manhattan	40 Wall St.	927	7
35	6	Citicorp	Lex. Av. & 54 St.	914	4
30	7	R.C.A.	Rockefeller Center	850	7
49	8	One Chase Man. Plaza	(Lower Manhattan)	813	6
44	9	Pan Am	200 Park Av.	808	5
21	10	Woolworth	233 Broadway	792	6
12	11	One Penn Plaza	33 St.	766	5
6	12	Exxon	1251 Av. of Americas	750	5
23	13	One Liberty Plaza (U.S. Steel)	(next to the World Trade Center)	743	5
27	14	Twenty Exchange Place	(Citibank)	741	5
9	15	One Astor Plaza	7 Av. at 45 St.	730	5
15	16	Union Carbide	270 Park Av.	707	5
29	17	General Motors	767 5 Av.	705	5
19	18	Metropolitan Life	1 Madison Av.	700	5
14	19	Five Hundred Fifth Avenue		697	6
28	20	Avon Products	9 West 57 St.	688	5
43	21	Chemical Bank, N.Y. Trust	277 Park Av.	687	5
54	22	Fifty-five Water St.	(Lower Manhattan)	687	5
42	23	Chanin	122 E. 42 St.	680	5
1	24	Gulf and Western	15 Columbus Circle	679	4
24	25	Marine Midland Bank	140 Broadway	677	5
8	26	McGraw-Hill	1221 Av. of Americas	674	5
45	27	Lincoln	60 East 42 St.	673	5
7	28	Sixteen-thirty-three Broadway		670	4
16	29	American Brands	245 Park Ave.	648	4
25	30	Irving Trust	1 Wall St.	640	5
32	31	Three-hundred-forty-five Park Av.		634	4
11	32	New York Telephone Co.	1095 Av. of Americas	630	4
50	33	Home Insurance Co.	60 John St.	630	4
55	34	One New York Plaza	(Lower Manhattan)	630	4
13	35	Grace Plaza (Monsanto)	1114 Av. of Americas	630	5
4	36	Eight-hundred-eighty-eight Seventh Ave.		628	4
38	37	One Hammarskjold Plaza	E. 47 St.	628	5
2	38	Burlington House	1345 Av. of Americas	625	5
39	39	Waldorf Astoria (Hotel)	301 Park Ave.	625	4
18	40	Ten East 40 St.		620	4
31	41	Olympic	645 5 Av.	620	5
34	42	General Electric	570 Lexington Av.	616	5
46	43	New York Life	51 Madison Av.	615	4
3	44	J.C. Penney	1301 Av. of Americas	609	4
40	45	Five-hundred-sixty Lexington Ave.		600	4
10	46	Celanese	1211 Av. of Americas	592	4
5	47	Time and Life	1271 Av. of Americas	587	4
20	48	Federal Building	Foley Sq. (Lower Manhattan)	587	4
47	49	Municipal Building	1 Centre St.	580	3
33	50	The Ritz	Park Av. and 57 St.	540	4
26	51	Bankers Trust	6 Wall St.	540	3
36	52	Random House	825 3rd Ave.	522	4
53	53	Bank of New York	48 Wall St.	513	3
48	54	United States Courthouse	Foley Square	505	4
37	55	United Nations Secretariat	E. 42 St.	505	4

SKYSCRAPERS

Alphabetical List

(For address, height and number of floors, see previous index)

Name	Number on map	Rank (in height)
American Brands	16	29
American International, see Sixty Wall Tower		
Avon Products	28	20
Bankers Trust	26	51
Bank of Manhattan	52	5
Bank of New York	53	53
Burlington House	2	39
Celanese	10	46
Chanin	42	23
Chemical Bank, N.Y. Trust	43	21
Chrysler	41	3
Citicorp	35	6
Eight hundred eighty-eight 7th Avenue	4	37
Empire State Building	17	2
Exxon	6	12
Federal Building	20	48
Fifty-five Water Street	54	22
Five hundred 5th Avenue	14	19
Five hundred sixty Lexington Avenue	40	45
General Electric	34	31
General Motors	29	17
Grace Plaza (Monsanto)	13	36
Gulf and Western	1	24
Home Insurance Co.	50	34
Irving Trust	25	30
J.C. Penney	3	44
Lincoln	45	27
Marine Midland	24	25
McGraw-Hill	8	26
Metropolitan Life	19	18
Municipal Building	47	49
New York Life	46	43
New York Telephone Co.	11	33
Olympic	31	42
One Astor Plaza	9	15
One Chase Manhattan	49	8
One Hammarskjold Plaza	38	38
One Liberty Plaza	23	13
One New York Plaza	55	35
One Penn Plaza	12	11
Pan Am	44	9
Random House	36	52
R.C.A.	30	7
Ritz, The	33	50
Sixteen thirty-three Broadway	7	28
Sixty Wall Tower	51	4
Ten East 40 St.	18	41
Three hundred forty-five Park Avenue	32	32
Time and Life	5	47
Twenty Exchange Place	27	14
Union Carbide	15	16
United Nations Secretariat	37	55
United States Courthouse	48	54
Uris, see Sixteen thirty-three Broadway		
Waldorf Astoria Hotel	39	40
Woolworth	21	10
World Trade Center	22	1

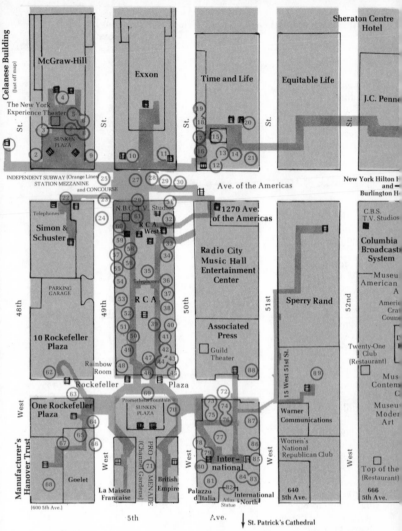

ROCKEFELLER CENTER and UNDERGROUND CONCOURSE
With Shops and Services

The numbers in circles are keys to index on next page.

STAIRS OR ESCALATORS 🏢   UNDERGROUND CONCOURSE AREA PASSAGEWAYS

(All named features (except subway concourse, sunken plazas, and the New York Experience Theater are located above the concourse level).

The Rockefeller Center Complex includes 19 buildings, covering 22 acres, and is used mainly for business. There are a total of 557 floors, almost 48,758 windows, and a working population of over 65,000 persons. The original center, which includes the R C A building, was completed in 1940.

Number on map

1 The Beanstalk Restaurant 997-1005
2 Cardio Fitness Center — 840-8240
3 The New York Experience 869-0346
4 Casella Pen & Gift Shop 869-9492
5 Ritter Travel Bureau — 869-3555
6 Concourse Tobacconist — 869-8988
7 B. Nelson/General Shoe Repair 869-3552
8 McGraw-Hill Book Store — 997-4100
9 Lamston's — 757-3430
10 Chemical Bank — 922-4156
11 La Petite Brasserie — 265-3545
12 Bon Jour Coffee Shop — 265-3545
13 Dawson's Pub — 265-3545
14 Cione's Hair Styling Salon 757-2561
15 Plymouth Poco — 873-5600
16 Photomart 50th Ltd. — 265-4245
17 Eastern Newsstand
18 Shay's Photostat Service — 265-2874
19 Brands Mart — 937-3600
20 Manufacturers Hanover Trust 350-6121
21 General Shoe Repair — 869-3552
22 Harris Florist — 246-6640
23 Fotomat — 541-5140
24 Quick Licks — 757-0496
25 Eastern Newsstand
26 Grand Gourmet — 541-5130
27 Nedick's — 560-8036
28 Little Nick Pizza — 974-9310
29 Take Home Shop — 765-8122
30 First Federal Savings & Loan 397-9849
31 Marvel Cleaners — 245-5343
32 Au Bon Pain — 541-8507
33 Fro-gurt Shoppe — 582-8092
34 General Shoe Repair — 869-3552
35 Plymouth Shop — 873-5600
36 Burger Train — 246-5807
37 Greengrocer's Pantry — 586-0132
38 Plymouth Shop — 873-5600
39 The Crepe Place — 246-5807
40 Hellenic Arts Center — 246-3670
41 Fanny Farmer Candies — 586-0869
42 Personally Yours—Bath/Closet 582-3381
43 Belmont Bird & Kennel Shop 247-0620
44 Manufacturers Hanover Trust 350-6316
45 International Newsstand
46 Party Bazaar—Cards & Gifts 581-0310
47 Plaza Jewelry & Gifts — 265-3137

Number on map

48 Anand India Shop — 247-2054
49 Photomart 49th Ltd. — 246-0465
50 Soeda Gift Shop — 265-7731
51 Plymouth Shop — 873-5600
52 Seki Inc. Jewelers — 582-3893
53 Step 'n Style Shoes — 757-6690
54 Dr. Barry S. Marquit — Podiatrist 246-3364
55 RMH International—Gifts 757-5535
56 La Parfumarie Marco — 586-8434
57 Manfra, Tordella & Brookes, Inc. 757-9670
58 Dr. Ronald Fields—Optometrist 247-7392
59 Ruth Hats & Handbags — 245-8924
60 Hong Kong House — 582-6592
61 The New York Bank for Savings 957-3785
62 Hamburger Center, U.S.A. 757-2455
63 Efficiency Beauty Center 245-8970
64 The Nook Restaurant — 757-6575
65 Datagraphix — 586-3411
66 Tobron Corp.—Office Furniture 586-2681
67 Travelroutes International 765-9778
68 Irene Hermann Lettershop 247-6671
69 Granny's Bag — 581-2453
70 Coffee Cafe — 974-4891
71 Promenade Cafe — 757-5730
72 Libraire de France — 673-7400
73 U.S. Post Office — 265-3854
74 Morgan Guaranty — 483-2323
75 East River Savings Bank 374-7700
76 Karann Boutique — 765-8161
77 Harmal Travel Service — 581-3634
78 Marvel Cleaners — 247-1522
79 Fiscella's Men's Hair Salon 246-3151
80 International Flower Shop 265-5644
81 B.G. Canevares Jewelers — 247-5644
82 Barclays Bank — 265-1105
83 Penn Office Supply — 246-6022
84 Amal Printing — 247-3270
85 American Cafeteria — 581-3580
86 Passport Acme Photo — 247-2911
87 General Shoe Repair — 869-3552
88 Old Times Restaurant — 581-3580
89 Bankers Trust — 775-2500
90 ITT World Communications 797-7530
91 Cosmos Ticket Office — 265-8600

DEPARTMENT STORES
and
SPECIALTY SHOPS

Midtown

Scale in feet

0   2000

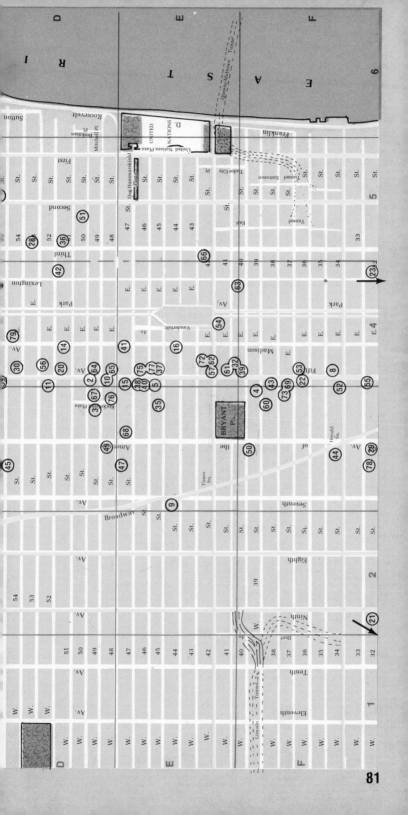

DEPARTMENT STORES AND SPECIALTY SHOPS

Number on map	Name	Address	Map key
1	Alexander's; 731 Lexington Av; dept store		C-4
2	Alfred Dunhill of London; 620 5th Av; tobacconists		D-4
3	Anand India Art Shop; 30 Rockefeller Plz; gifts		D-3
4	Arnold Constable; 1 W 39th St.; dept store		F-3
5	Arthur Brown & Bro.; 2 W 46th St; artist's materials		E-3
6	Azuma; 666 Lexington Av; gifts		C-4
7	Baccarat; 55 E 57th St; giftware		C-4
8	B. Altman; 5th Av & 34th St; dept store		F-4
9	Barnes & Noble; 1521 Broadway; books		E-3
10	Barnes & Noble; 5th Av & 48th St; bookstore		D-4
11	B. Dalton; 666 5th Av; bookseller		D-3
12	Bergdorf Goodman; 754 5th Av; dept store		C-4
13	Bloomingdale's; 1000 3rd Av; dept store		C-4
14	British American House; 488 Madison Av; rainwear		D-4
15	Brentano's; 586 5th Av; books		E-4
16	Brooks Bros.; 346 Madison Av; men's clothing		E-4
17	Cardel Ltd.; 615 Madison Av; china		C-4
18	Carey Fabrics; 2286 Broadway; fabrics (off map)		
19	Carole Stupell; 61 E 57th St; table settings		C-4
20	Cartier; 5th Av & 52nd St; jewelry		D-4
21	Classic Bookshop; 248 World Trade Center Concourse; books (off map in lower Manhattan)		F-2
22	Dennison; 390 5th Av; party goods		F-4
23	Deutsch Inc.; 196 Lexington Av; wicker furniture		F-4
24	Doubleday Book Shops; 724 5th Av; 673 5th Av; books		C-4
25	Dunhill Tailored Clothes; 65 E 57th St; men's clothes		C-4
26	F.A.O. Schwarz; 745 5th Av; toys		C-4
27	Fioravanti, Wm.; 45 W. 57th St; men's tailors		C-3
28	Fortunoff; 681 5th Av; jewelry		D-5
29	Gimbels; 33rd St & Broadway; dept store		F-3
30	Gucci Shops; 689 5th Av; shoes		D-4
31	Hammacher Schlemmer; 147 E 57th St; gifts		C-4
32	Hammond Map Store Inc.; 12 E 41st St; maps		E-4
33	Harry Winston Inc.; 718 5th Av; jewelry		C-4
34	Henri Bendel Inc.; 10 W 57 St; women's clothes		C-3
35	Herbert Gladson, Ltd.; 45 W 45th St; fabrics		E-3
36	Herman's World of Sporting Goods; 845 3rd Av; sporting goods		D-5
37	Hoffritz For Cutlery; 30 Rockefeller Plaza ; cutlery		E-4
38	International Jewelry Exchange Assoc.; 578 5th Av; jewelry		E-4
39	Lane Bryant; 465 5th Av; women's clothes		F-4
40	Larousse & Co.; 572 5th Av; books		E-3
41	Lefcourt Shoes Inc.; 400 Madison Av; men's shoes		E-4
42	Lexington Flower Shop; 595 Lexington Av; florist		D-4
43	Lord & Taylor; 424 5th Av; dept store		F-4
44	Macy's; Herald Sq.; dept store		F-3
45	Make-Up Center, The; 150 W 55th St; cosmetics		D-3
46	Manhattan Art & Antiques Center; 1050 2nd Av; antiques		D-5
47	Manny's Musical Instruments & Accessories, Inc.; 156 W 48th St; musical instruments		E-3
48	Maximilian Fur Co.; 20 W 57th St.; furs		C-3
49	McGraw-Hill Bookstore; 1221 Av of the Americas; books		D-3
50	Nature Food Centers; 1055 Av of the Americas; 1273 Lexington Av; health food		F-3

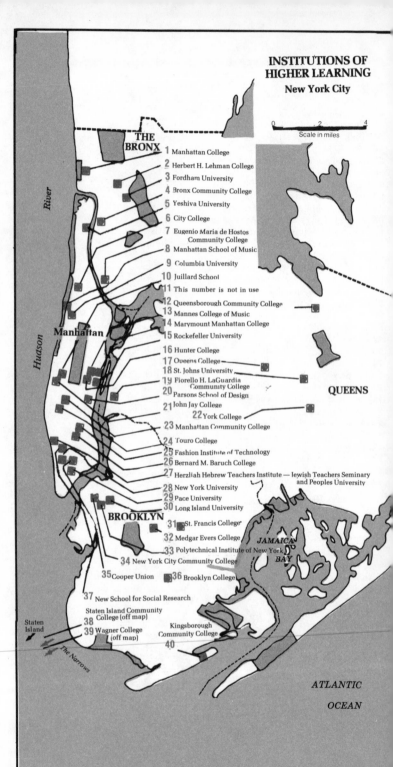

INSTITUTIONS OF HIGHER LEARNING
New York City

0   2   4
Scale in miles

THE BRONX

1 Manhattan College
2 Herbert H. Lehman College
3 Fordham University
4 Bronx Community College
5 Yeshiva University
6 City College
7 Eugenio Maria de Hostos Community College
8 Manhattan School of Music
9 Columbia University
10 Juilliard School
11 This number is not in use
12 Queensborough Community College
13 Mannes College of Music
14 Marymount Manhattan College
15 Rockefeller University
16 Hunter College
17 Queens College
18 St. Johns University
19 Fiorello H. LaGuardia Community College
20 Parsons School of Design
21 John Jay College
22 York College
23 Manhattan Community College
24 Touro College
25 Fashion Institute of Technology
26 Bernard M. Baruch College
27 Herzliah Hebrew Teachers Institute — Jewish Teachers Seminary and Peoples University
28 New York University
29 Pace University
30 Long Island University
31 St. Francis College
32 Medgar Evers College
33 Polytechnic Institute of New York
34 New York City Community College
35 Cooper Union
36 Brooklyn College
37 New School for Social Research
38 Staten Island Community College (off map)
39 Wagner College (off map)
40 Kingsborough Community College

Manhattan

Hudson River

Hudson

QUEENS

BROOKLYN

JAMAICA BAY

Staten Island

The Narrows

ATLANTIC OCEAN

Number on Map		Address	Borough
26	Bernard M Baruch College	17 Lexington Ave	Manhattan
4	Bronx Community College	Univ Ave & 181 St	Bronx
36	Brooklyn College	Bedford Av & Ave H	Brooklyn
6	City College	Convent Ave & W 138 St	Manhattan
	College of Insurance	123 William St	Manhattan
9	Columbia University	116 St & Broadway	Manhattan
35	Cooper Union	41 Cooper Sq.	Manhattan
25	Fashion Inst. of Technology	227 W 27th St	Manhattan
3	Fordham University	E. Fordham Rd & 3 Ave	Bronx
27	Herzliah Hebrew Teachers Inst.— Jewish Teachers Seminary and Peoples University	69 Bank St	Manhattan
7	Hostos, Eugenio Maria de Community College	475 Grand Concourse	Bronx
16	Hunter College	695 Park Ave	Manhattan
21	John Jay College	445 W 59 St	Manhattan
10	Juilliard School	Lincoln Center Plz	Manhattan
40	Kingsborough Community College	2001 Oriental Blvd	Brooklyn
19	Fiorello H. LaGuardia Community College	31-10 Thomson Ave	Queens
2	Lehman, Herbert H., College	Bedford Pk Blvd & Goulden Av	Bronx
30	Long Island University	385 Flatbush Ave Ext	Brooklyn
1	Manhattan College	Man Coll Pkwy & W 242 St	Bronx
23	Manhattan Community College	1633 Broadway	Manhattan
8	Manhattan School of Music	120 Clarmont Av	Manhattan
13	Mannes College of Music	157 E 74th St	Manhattan
14	Marymount Manhattan College	221 E 71st St	Manhattan
32	Medgar Evers College	1150 Carroll St	Brooklyn
37	New School of Social Research	66 W 12 St	Manhattan
34	New York City Community College	300 Jay St	Brooklyn
28	New York University	Washington Sq	Manhattan
29	Pace University	Pace Plaza	Manhattan
20	Parsons School of Design	560 7th Ave	Manhattan
33	Polytechnic Institute of N.Y.	333 Jay St	Brooklyn
17	Queens College	65-30 Kissena Blvd	Queens
12	Queensborough Community College	Springfield Blvd & 56th Ave	Queens
15	Rockefeller University	1230 York Ave at 66 St	Manhattan
31	St. Francis College	180 Remsen Ave	Brooklyn
18	St. Jo' University	Grand Central Pkwy & Utopia Pkwy	Queens
38	...island Community ...ege	715 Ocean Terrace, Sunnyside	Richmond
24	...o College	30 W 44th St	Manhattan
39	Wagner College	631 Howard Ave	Richmond
5	Yeshiva University	500 W 185th St	Manhattan
22	York College	150-14 Jamaica Ave	Queens

JOGGING, BICYCLING AND ROLLER SKATING
IN NEW YORK CITY

Manhattan

Bicycling and jogging are excellent in Central Park, especially north of the lake, between the lake and Croton Reservoir. Another good route, best for jogging only, is in Riverside Park, from 125 St. south to 72 St. Even better for jogging are the paths in Ft. Tryon Park and Inwood Hill Park. If you like roughing it and climbing while jogging, try the paths along the eastern face of Morningside Park cliffs; but daytime only. Downtown locations include all of Washington Square Park, and along East River Park.

Bronx

The best routes for both jogging and bicycling are in Pelham Bay Park, especially on Hunters Island. Van Cortlandt Park, parts of Riverdale community and parts of Bronx Park have good jogging routes. Short stretches of Hutchinson River Pkwy. and Bronx River Pkwy. service roads are good for bicycling and jogging. But these cannot be used, or should not be used during high-traffic hours.

Queens

The best areas for jogging, bicycling and roller skating are in Flushing Meadows Park, and in the connecting units leading to Cunningham Park, by way of Kissena Corridor Pk. Bicycling paths exist in Forest Park, along South Parkway, and in Brookville Park. Utopia Pkwy., 164 St. and Little Neck Pkwy. have good stretches for jogging and bicycling. Another area is the service road of Van Wyck Expressway, southern portion only. The Rockaway Boardwalk is great for jogging but bicycles are not permitted there.

Brooklyn

Excellent jogging and bicycling paths are located along Belt Parkway (Shore Parkway), both east and west of Coney Island. The two sections are each about five miles long. Prospect Park has good roller skating surfaces, and is excellent for jogging. Highland Park is good for jogging. The service road of Kings Highway and of Linden Boulevard, at low-traffic times have excellent stretches for all three activities.

Staten Island

Bicycling and jogging routes are plentiful on Staten Island. Especially are Latourette, Todt Hill, Willow Brook, and Clove Lakes areas. Oceanside jogging could not be better — there are two four-mile stretches in the Gateway National Recreation Area beach section, from South Beach to Midland Beach, and Great Kills Park.

Roller Skating

Roller skating is not "kid stuff" any more. It's a big-time sport, both indoor and outdoor. It is fun, too, for exercising and skating on the streets and sidewalks. In the summer months thousands of New Yorkers regularly attach wheels to their feet.

For indoor roller skating, two of the best are Empire Rollerdome and Park Circle Rink, both in Brooklyn (see the Yellow Pages).

In Manhattan, there is Metropolis, at 241 West 55 St. (586-4649). But its a private club. Better for occasional indoor skating are Village Skating at 15 Waverly Place and Wednesday's Restaurant, 210 East 86 St.

On the outside, the best places are the great open plazas, such as those at World Trade Center, at Lincoln Plaza, and a large number of big skyscraper plazas along Ave. of the Americas and Park Ave.

The Central Park Roadways, when they are closed to traffic, and the Wollman Rink in that park are available for skating in the summer. The best streets for roller skating are in the Wall Street Area on weekends and during summer evenings.

Also good are The Avenue of Americas bike lane, and Amsterdam Ave. between 52 and 72 Sts. Many streets in Greenwich Village are great for skating, but the best area there is Washington Square Park.

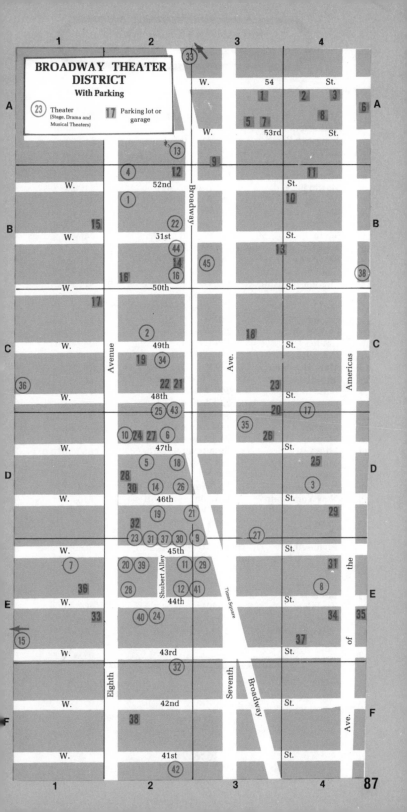

BROADWAY THEATER DISTRICT
With Parking

23 Theater
(Stage, Drama and
Musical Theaters)

17 Parking lot or garage

BROADWAY THEATERS
(Stage, Drama and Musical Theaters)

Number on map	Name	Address	Phone	Map key
1	Alvin	250 West 52 St.	757-8646	B-2
2	Ambassador	215 West 49 St.	541-6490	C-2
3	American Place	111 West 46 St.	243-0393	D-4
4	ANTA	245 West 52 St.	246-6270	B-2
5	Brooks Atkinson	256 West 47 St.	245-3430	D-2
6	Ethel Barrymore	243 West 47 St.	246-0390	D-2
7	Martin Beck	302 West 45 St.	246-6363	E-1
8	Belasco	111 West 44 St.	354-4490	E-4
9	Bijou	209 West 45 St.	221-8500	E-3
10	Biltmore	261 West 47 St.	582-5340	D-2
11	Booth	222 West 45 St.	246-5969	E-2
12	Broadhurst	235 West 44 St.	247-0472	E-2
13	Broadway	1681 Broadway	247-3600	A-2
14	Century	235 West 46 St.	354-6644	D-2
15	Chelsea Westside	407 West 43 St. (off the map)	974-9032	E-1
16	Circle in the Square	1633 Broadway	581-3270	B-2
17	Cort	138 West 48 St.	489-6392	C-4
18	Edison	240 West 47 St.	757-7164	D-2
19	Forty-sixth St.	226 West 46 St.	246-0246	D-2
20	Golden	252 West 45 St.	246-6740	E-2
21	Helen Hayes	210 West 46 St.	246-6380	D-2
22	Mark Hellinger	237 West 51 St.	757-7064	B-2
23	Imperial	249 West 45 St.	265-4311	E-2
24	Little	240 West 44 St.	221-6425	E-2
25	Longacre	220 West 48 St.	246-5639	D-2
26	Lunt-Fontanne	205 West 46 St.	586-5555	D-2
27	Lyceum	149 West 45 St.	582-3897	D-3
28	Majestic	245 West 44 St.	246-0730	E-2
29	Minskoff	Broadway & 45 St.	869-0550	E-3
30	Morosco	217 West 45 St.	246-6230	E-2
31	Music Box	239 West 45 St.	246-4636	E-2
32	New Apollo	234 West 43 St.	921-8558	F-2
33	New York State	Lincoln Center (off map)	870-5500	A-2
34	Eugene O'Neill	230 West 49 St.	246-0220	C-2
35	Palace	1564 Broadway	757-2626	D-3
36	Playhouse	359 West 48 St.	489-9237	C-1
37	Plymouth	236 West 45 St.	730-1760	E-2
38	Radio City Music Hall	1260 Ave. of the Americas	582-8370	B-2
39	Royale	242 West 45 St.	245-5760	E-2
40	St. James	246 West 44 St.	398-0280	E-2
41	Shubert	225 West 44 St.	246-5990	E-
42	Trafalgar	208 West 41 St.	921-8000	F-2
43	Uris	1633 Broadway	586-6510	B-
44	Winter Garden	1634 Broadway	245-4878	B-

THEATER DISTRICT PARKING

(Prices range from minimum of $3.00 to a maximum of $9.00)

Number on map	Address	Owner	Phone	Map Key
	54th - 55th sts.			
1	156 West 54 St.	Kinney	997-9695	A-3
2	138 West 54 St.	Kinney	997-9694	A-4
3	100 West 54 St.	Kinney	889-4444	A-4
4	100 West 55 St.	Ziegfeld Garage	582-4714	A-4
	52nd - 53rd sts.			
5	159 West 53 St.	Kinney	997-9694	A-3
6	1330 Ave. of the Americas	Meyers	586-0169	A-4
7	141 West 53 St.	Kinney	560-8010	A-3
8	101 West 53 St.	Kinney	586-7000	A-4
9	810 7th Ave.	Square Parking	974-9317	A-3
10	130 West 52 St.	Square Parking	247-3261	B-4
11	125 West 52 St.	Edison	974-9387	B-4
12	52 St. & Broadway	Edison	840-8791	B-2
	50th - 51st sts.			
13	140 West 51 St.	Tower Parking	560-8232	B-3
14	1633 Broadway	Meyers	997-9522	B-2
15	301 West 51 St.	Kinney	581-4100	B-1
16	814-826 8th Ave.	Edison	997-9567	B-2
17	300 West 50 St.	Square Parking	974-9326	C-1
	48th - 49th sts.			
18	149 West 49 St.	Meyers	974-9838	C-3
19	254 West 49 St.	Kinney	581-7000	C-2
20	148 West 48 St.	Sun Garage	575-9133	C-3
21	215 West 48 St.	President	245-9628	C-2
22	235 West 48 St.	Kinney	997-4042	C-2
23	155 West 48 St.	Kinney	997-9773	C-3
	46th - 47th sts.			
24	257 West 47 St.	W. 47 St. Garage	664-9602	D-2
25	114 West 47 St.	Square Parking	730-9014	D-4
26	145 West 47 St.	Meyers	730-9387	D-3
27	253 West 47 St.	Kinney	997-9414	D-2
28	754 8th Ave.	Edison	730-9117	D-2
29	102 West 46 St.	Gotham	245-9592	D-4
30	225 West 46 St.	Edison	221-9731	D-2
	42nd - 45th sts.			
31	102 West 45 St.	Kinney	· 560-8661	E-4
32	251 West 45 St.	Bowser 45th	974-9825	F-2
33	306 West 44 St.	Square Parking	247-5807	E-1
34	100 West 44 St.	Kinney	730-9184	E-4
35	50 West 44 St.	Hippodrome	560-9241	E-4
36	307 West 44 St.	Edison	974-9830	E-1
37	141 West 43 St.	Meyers	730-9002	E-4
38	264 West 42 St.	Square Parking	764-9026	F-2

OFF-BROADWAY THEATERS

Midtown and Uptown

The scale of this map has been distorted in an east-west direction only. Therefore, the island appears to be wider than it really is. This is done to give more space for information on the map.

INWOOD HILL PK.

FT. TRYON PK.

HIGH BRIDGE PK.

RIVERSIDE PK.

CENTRAL PARK

RANDALLS ISLAND

WARDS I.

1 Equity Library

2 Beacon

3 78 St. Theater

4 Vivian Beaumont

5 Avery Fisher Hall

6 New York City Opera

7 Alice Tully Hall

8 Julliard

9 Royal Court Repertory

10 Cubiculo

11 No Smoking Playhouse

12 Harold Clurman

13 Manhattan Punchline

14 Troupe City Ltd.

15 Hudson Guild

Three Muses   16
Metropolitan Opera   17
Eastside Playhouse   18
Manhattan
  Theater Club   19
Marymount Manhattan   20
  Theater Four   21
Theater East   22
ROOSEVELT I.
Carnegie Hall   23
St. Peter's Church
  Theater   24
The Phoenix   25
Quaigh   26
Town Hall   27

Roundabout Stage One

EAST RIVER PK.

Hudson River

WEST SIDE HIGHWAY

WASHINGTON SQ. PK.

Houston

Delancey St.

Canal St.

Grand St.

Brooklyn Br.

City Hall PK.

Fulton St.

Wall St.

Battery Pk.

East River   28

The West Side Highway (an elevated, limited-access roadway) has been closed to all traffic south of 46 St. for an indefinite period, pending completion of plans to reconstruct and reroute the highway.   West St. and Twelfth Av. can be used for through traffic.

90

OFF-BROADWAY THEATERS
(Drama, Musical and Stage Theaters)

MIDTOWN AND UPTOWN

Number on map	Name	Address	Phone
	Alice Tully Hall	Lincoln Center*	362-1911
	Avery Fisher Hall	Lincoln Center	874-2424
	Beacon	2124 Broadway	874-1717
	Carnegie Hall	154 West 57 St.	247-7459
	Harold Clurman Theater	412 West 42 St.	594-2370
	Cubiculo	414 West 51 St.	265-2138
	Eastside Playhouse Co.	334 East 74 St.	861-2288
	Equity Library Theater	103 St. and Riverside Dr.	663-2028
	Hudson Guild	441 West 26 St.	760-9810
	Julliard	Lincoln Center	799-5000
	Manhattan Punchline	260 West 41 St.	921-8288
	Manhattan Theater Club	321 East 73 St.	288-2500
	Marymount Manhattan	221 East 71 St.	737-9611
	Metropolitan Opera	Lincoln Center	580-9830
	New York City Opera	Lincoln Center	877-4700
	No Smoking Playhouse	354 West 45 St.	582-7862
	Phoenix, The	1540 Broadway	730-0787
	Quaigh	110 West 43 St.	221-9088
	Roundabout Stage One	333 West 23 St.	924-7160
	Royal Court Repertory	301 West 55 St.	997-9582
	78 St. Theater Lab.	236 West 78 St.	595-0850
	St. Peter's Church Theater	Lex. Av. at 54 St.	751-4140
	Theater East	211 East 60 St.	838-0177
	Theater Four	424 West 55 St.	246-8545
	Town Hall	123 West 43 St.	840-2824
	Three Muses Theater	2109 Broadway	874-1279
	Troupe City, Ltd.	335 West 39 St.	244-9699
	Vivian Beaumont	Lincoln Center	787-6868

* Lincoln Center is located at Broadway and West 65 St.

OFF-BROADWAY
THEATERS
Greenwich Village
East Village

Scale
0   1/4
Miles

JACOB RIIS HOUSES

The West Side Highway (an elevated, limited-access road) has been closed to all traffic for an indefinite period, pending completion of plans to reconstruct and reroute the highway. West Street and Twelfth Ave. can both be used for through traffic.

OFF-BROADWAY THEATERS
(Drama, Musical and Stage Theaters)

GREENWICH VILLAGE

Number on Map	Name	Address	Phone	Map key
1	Abbey Theater	136 East 13 St.	677-4210	B-4
2	Actor's Playhouse	100 7 Av. South	691-6226	B-2
3	Astor Place	434 Lafayette St.	254-4370	C-4
4	Bouwerie Lane Theater	330 Bowery	677-0060	D-4
5	Cherry Lane Theater	38 Commerce St.	989-2020	D-2
6	Circle in the Square	159 Bleecker St.	254-6330	D-3
7	Circle Repertory Co.	99 7 Av. South	924-7100	B-3
8	CSC Repertory Co.	136 East 13 St.	677-4210	B-3
9	Entermedia Theater	189 2 Av.	475-4101	B-5
10	La Ma Ma Experimental	74A East 4 St.	475-7710	C-4
11	Orpheum	126 2 Av.	260-2625	C-5
12	Performing Garage	33 Wooster St.	966-3651	D-3
13	Players Theater	115 Macdougal St.	254-5076	C-3
14	Province Town Playhouse	133 Macdougal	777-2571	C-3
15	Public Theater	425 Lafayette St.	598-7100	C-4
16	Rediculous Theater	1 Sheridan Square	260-7137	C-3
17	St. Marks Playhouse	133 2 Av.	533-9292	C-5
18	Shandol	137 West 22 St.	243-9504	A-3
19	Shelter West	217 2nd Av	673-6341	D-3
20	Soho Repertory	19 Mercer St.	929-2588	D-4
21	Squat Theater	256 West 23 St.	691-1238	A-2
22	Theater for the New City	162 2 Av.	254-1109	B-5
23	Sullivan St. Playhouse	181 Sullivan St.	674-3838	D-3
24	Thirteenth St.	50 West 13 St.	741-9282	B-3
25	Theater De Lys	121 Christopher St.	924-8782	D-2
26	Truck and Warehouse	79 East 4 St.	228-8558	C-4
27	Village Gate	160 Bleecker St.	475-5120	D-3

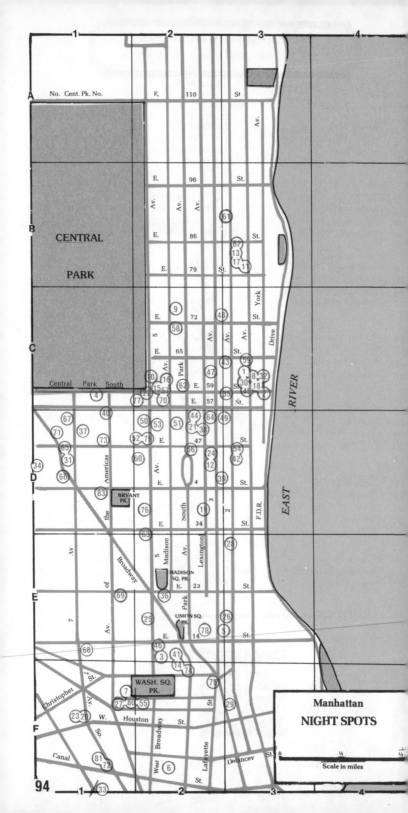

Manhattan
NIGHT SPOTS

Scale in miles

94

Number on map	Name, Address, Phone	Map Key
1	Adam's Apple, 1117 1st Av; 371-8650; Disco	C-3
2	Ali-Baba East, 400 E. 59 St; 688-4710	C-3
3	Asti, 13 E 12 St; 741-9105; Operatic Arias	E-3
4	Barbizon Plaza Library, 106 Central Park S; 247-7000; Disco	C-1
5	Blue Hawaii, 135 3rd Av; 260-7690	E-3
6	Boltax, 22 Wooster; 226-4487; Cabaret	F-2
7	Bottom Line Cabaret Theatre, 15 W 4th St; 228-6300; Top Recording Acts	F-1
8	Cachaca, 403 E 62 St; 688-8501; Brazilian Entertainment	C-3
9	Cafe Carlyle (in Carlyle Hotel), 35 E 76 St; 744-1600; Music/Dancing	C-2
10	Cafe Pierre (in Pierre Hotel), 5th Av & 61 St; 838-8000; Music/Dancing	C-2
11	Catch A Rising Star, 1487 1st Av; 794-1906	B-3
12	Chateau Madrid, 48 St & Lexington Av, 752-8080; Top Shows/Dancing	D-2
13	Comic Strip, 1568 2nd Av; 861-9386; Comedy Club	B-3
14	Cookery, The, 8th St & University Pl; 674-4450; Jazz/Blues	F-2
15	Copa Disco, 10 E 60 St; 755-6010	C-2
16	Copacabana, 10 E 60 St; 755-6010; Entertainment	C-2
17	Court Street Discotheque, 1544 2nd Av; 535-3394	B-3
18	Dangerfields, 1118 1st Av; 593-1650; Shows	C-3
19	David Copperfield, 322 Lexington Av; 684-8227	D-2
20	Duplex, The, 55 Grove; 255-5438; Cabaret	F-1
21	Eddie Condon Club, 144 W 54 St; 265-8277; Jazz	D-2
22	Edwardian Room (in Plaza Hotel), W 59 St & 5th Av; 759-3000; Dancing	C-2
23	El Avram, 80 Grove St; 243-0602/9661; Israeli-Mediterranean Kosher Club	F-1
24	El-Sultan (at Ibis), 151 E 50 St; 753-3471; Belly Dancers/Shows	D-3
25	Electric Circus, 100 5th Av; 989-7457; Disco	E-2
26	Fat Tuesday's, 190 3rd Av; 533-7902; Jazz	E-3
27	Folk City, 130 W 3rd St; 254-8449; Mon: Hootennany; Tue: Jazz; Wed & Thur: Rock/Country/Pop; Fri thru Sun: Folk/Rock	F-1
28	Good Times, 449 3rd Av; 686-4250	E-3
29	Great Gildersleeves, The, 331 Bowery, 533-3940; Rock and Roll	F-3
30	Gregory's, 1149 1st Av; 371-2220; Jazz	C-3
31	Hawaii Kai, 1638 Broadway; 757-0900; Dancing/Shows	D-1
32	Hippopotamus, 405 E 62 St; 486-1566; Cabaret/Disco	C-3
33	Hors D'Oeuvrerie, 1 World Trade Center (off map); 938-1111; Jazz/Dancing	F-1
34	Improvisation, 358 W 44 St; 765-8268; Show-Case Club	D-1
35	Jacques, 210 E 58 St; 753-5513; Hungarian/Gypsy Orchestra	C-3
36	Jazzmania Society, 14 E 23 St; 477-3077	E-2

96

Box office (212) 293-4300

YANKEE STADIUM

Located at River Ave. and 161st St.,
Bronx, N.Y. 10451

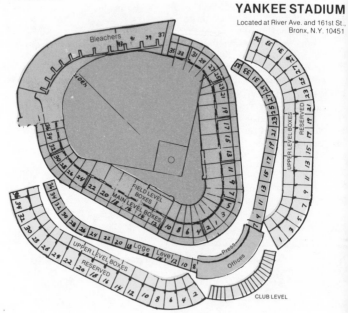

SHEA STADIUM

Located at 126th street at Roosevelt Ave.,
Flushing, N.Y. 11368

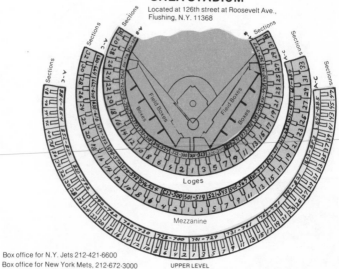

Box office for N.Y. Jets 212-421-6600
Box office for New York Mets, 212-672-3000

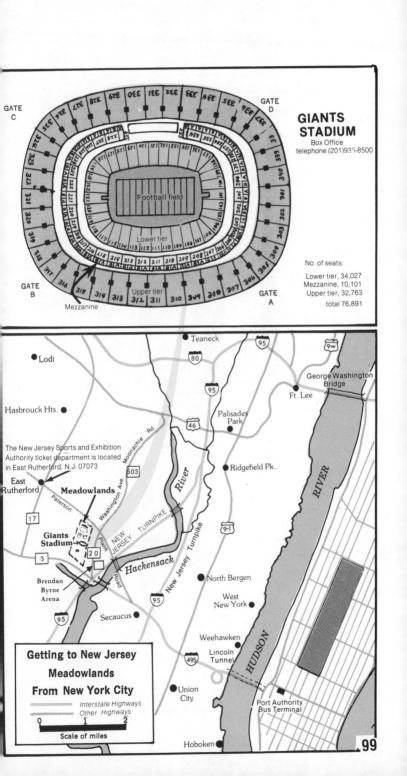

GIANTS STADIUM
Box Office telephone (201)935-8500

GATE C

GATE D

Football field

Lower tier

Mezzanine

GATE B

Upper tier

Mezzanine

GATE A

No. of seats:

Lower tier, 34,027
Mezzanine, 10,101
Upper tier, 32,763
total 76,891

Lodi

Teaneck

George Washington Bridge

Ft. Lee

Hasbrouck Hts.

Palisades Park

The New Jersey Sports and Exhibition Authority ticket department is located in East Rutherford, N.J. 07073

Ridgefield Pk.

East Rutherford

Meadowlands

Giants Stadium

Brendan Byrne Arena

North Bergen

West New York

Secaucus

Weehawken

Lincoln Tunnel

Union City

Port Authority Bus Terminal

Hoboken

Getting to New Jersey Meadowlands From New York City

Interstate Highways
Other Highways

0   1   2

Scale of miles

99

HOSPITALS, CLINICS AND MEDICAL CENTERS

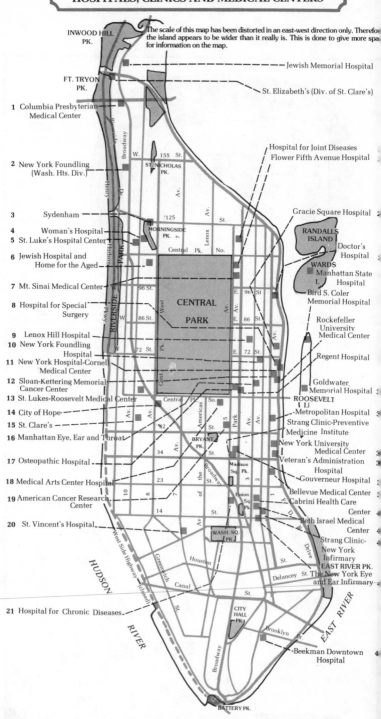

The scale of this map has been distorted in an east-west direction only. Therefor the island appears to be wider than it really is. This is done to give more spa for information on the map.

INWOOD HILL PK.

FT. TRYON PK.

Jewish Memorial Hospital

St. Elizabeth's (Div. of St. Clare's)

1 Columbia Presbyterian Medical Center

2 New York Foundling (Wash. Hts. Div.)

Hospital for Joint Diseases
Flower Fifth Avenue Hospital

3 Sydenham

Gracie Square Hospital

4 Woman's Hospital
5 St. Luke's Hospital Center

RANDALLS ISLAND

Doctor's Hospital

WARDS I.

6 Jewish Hospital and Home for the Aged

Manhattan State Hospital

7 Mt. Sinai Medical Center

Bird S. Coler Memorial Hospital

8 Hospital for Special Surgery

Rockefeller University Medical Center

9 Lenox Hill Hospital
10 New York Foundling Hospital

Regent Hospital

11 New York Hospital-Cornell Medical Center

12 Sloan-Kettering Memorial Cancer Center

Goldwater Memorial Hospital

13 St. Lukes-Roosevelt Medical Center

ROOSEVELT I.I.

14 City of Hope

Metropolitan Hospital

15 St. Clare's

Strang Clinic-Preventive Medicine Institute

16 Manhattan Eye, Ear and Throat

New York University Medical Center

17 Osteopathic Hospital

Veteran's Administration Hospital

Gouverneur Hospital

18 Medical Arts Center Hospital

Bellevue Medical Center

19 American Cancer Research Center

Cabrini Health Care Center

20 St. Vincent's Hospital

Beth Israel Medical Center

Strang Clinic-New York Infirmary

EAST RIVER PK.

The New York Eye and Ear Infirmary

21 Hospital for Chronic Diseases

Beekman Downtown Hospital

CENTRAL PARK

HUDSON RIVER

EAST RIVER

100

HOSPITALS, CLINICS AND MEDICAL RESEARCH CENTERS
Manhattan

mber map	Name	Address	Phone
9	American Cancer Research Center	516 5 Av.	840-2585
4	Beekman Downtown Hospital	170 William St.	233-5300
9	Bellevue Medical Center	27 St. & 1 Av.	561-5151
1	Beth Israel Medical Center	307 2 Av.	420-2139
0	Bird S. Coler Memorial Hospital	Roosevelt Is.	688-9400
0	Cabrini Health Care Center	227 E. 19 St.	725-6000
4	City of Hope	250 W. 57 St.	582-3030
1	Columbia Presbyterian Med. Ctr.	622 W. 168 St.	694-2500
	Columbus Hospital, see Cabrini Health Care Center		
8	Doctor's Hospital	170 East End Av.	535-3000
6	Flower Fifth Av. Hospital	5 Av. at 106 St.	860-8000
3	Goldwater Memorial Hospital	Roosevelt Island	750-6705
8	Gouverneur Hospital	227 Madison Av.	374-4000
7	Gracie Square Hospital	420 E. 76 St.	988-4400
1	Hospital for Chronic Diseases	119 5 Av.	982-2292
5	Hospital for Joint Diseases	1824 Madison Av.	348-4411
8	Hospital for Special Surgery	535 E. 70 St.	535-5500
6	Jewish Hospital and Home for the Aged	120 W. 106 St.	666-2000
2	Jewish Memorial Hospital	Broadway & 196 St.	569-4700
9	Lenox Hill Hospital	77 St. & Park Av.	794-4567
	Leroy Division, see Osteopathic Hospital		
6	Manhattan Eye, Ear and Throat	210 E. 64 St.	838-9200
9	Manhattan State Hospital	Ward's Island	369-0500
8	Medical Arts Center Hospital	57 W. 57 St.	755-0200
4	Metropolitan Hospital	1901 1 Av.	360-6262
7	Mt. Sinai Medical Center	5 Av. & 100 St.	650-6500
3	New York Eye and Ear Infirmary	310 E. 14 St.	598-1313
0	New York Foundling Hospital	1173 3 Av.	879-2200
2	New York Foundling Hospital Washington Hts. Div.	611 W. 152 St.	862-3427
1	New York Hospital-Cornell Med. Ctr.	525 E. 68 St.	472-5000
6	New York University Medical Ctr.	560 1 Av.	679-3200
7	Osteopathic Hospital	40 E. 61 St.	838-8200
2	Regent Hospital	115 E. 61 St.	838-7200
1	Rockefeller University Med. Ctr.	1230 York Av.	360-1000
5	St. Clare's Hospital & Health Ctr.	415 W. 51 St.	586-1500
23	St. Elizabeth's Hospital (Div. of St. Clare's)	689 Ft. Wash. Av.	690-7600
5	St. Luke's Hospital Center	Amsterdam & 114 St	876-6000
3	St. Luke's-Roosevelt Hospital Ctr.	9 Av. & 59 St.	554-7000
20	St. Vincent's Hospital & Med. Ctr. of NY	7 Av. & W. 11 St.	790-7000
2	Sloan-Kettering Memorial	1275 York Av	794-7000
2	Strang Clinic-New York Infirmary	321 E. 15 St.	228-8000
5	Strang Clinic-Preventive Medicine Inst.	55 E. 34 St.	683-1000
3	Sydenham Hospital	565 Manhattan Av.	678-5151
7	Veteran's Administration Hospital	1 Av. & 24 St.	686-7500
4	Woman's Hospital	111 Amsterdam Av	870-6000

HOUSES OF WORSHIP

The scale of this map has been distorted in an east-west direction only. Therefor the island appears to be wider than it really is. This is done to give more spa for information on the map.

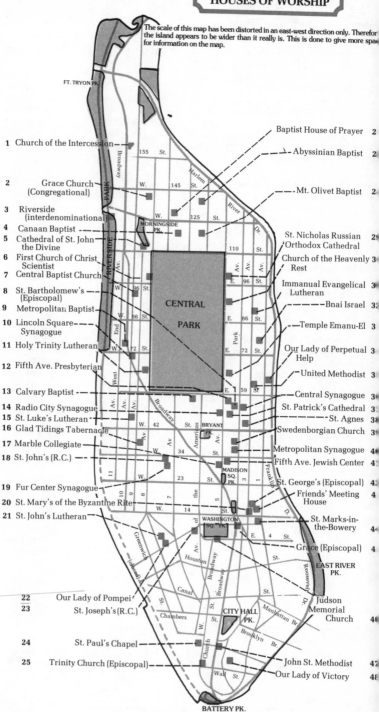

1 Church of the Intercession

2 Grace Church (Congregational)

3 Riverside (interdenominational)

4 Canaan Baptist

5 Cathedral of St. John the Divine

6 First Church of Christ Scientist

7 Central Baptist Church

8 St. Bartholomew's (Episcopal)

9 Metropolitan Baptist

10 Lincoln Square Synagogue

11 Holy Trinity Lutheran

12 Fifth Ave. Presbyterian

13 Calvary Baptist

14 Radio City Synagogue

15 St. Luke's Lutheran

16 Glad Tidings Tabernacle

17 Marble Collegiate

18 St. John's (R.C.)

19 Fur Center Synagogue

20 St. Mary's of the Byzantine Rite

21 St. John's Lutheran

22 Our Lady of Pompei

23 St. Joseph's (R.C.)

24 St. Paul's Chapel

25 Trinity Church (Episcopal)

Baptist House of Prayer 2

Abyssinian Baptist 2

Mt. Olivet Baptist 2

St. Nicholas Russian Orthodox Cathedral 2

Church of the Heavenly Rest 3

Immanual Evangelical Lutheran 3

Bnai Israel 32

Temple Emanu-El 3

Our Lady of Perpetual Help 3

United Methodist 3

Central Synagogue 3

St. Patrick's Cathedral 3

St. Agnes 3

Swedenborgian Church 3

Metropolitan Synagogue 40

Fifth Ave. Jewish Center 41

St. George's (Episcopal) 42

Friends' Meeting House 4

St. Marks-in-the-Bowery 44

Grace (Episcopal) 4

Judson Memorial Church 46

John St. Methodist 47

Our Lady of Victory 48

102

HOUSES OF WORSHIP

Number on map	Name	Address
27	Abyssinian Baptist Church, The	132 W. 38 St.
26	Baptist House of Prayer	80 W. 126 St.
32	Bnai Israel Congregation	335 E. 77 St.
13	Calvary Baptist Church	123 W. 57 St.
4	Canaan Baptist Church	132 W. 116 St.
7	Central Baptist Church	Amsterdam Av. & 92 St.
36	Central Synagogue	123 E. 65 St.
1	Church of the Intercession	550 W. 155 St.
41	Fifth Ave. Jewish Center	18 E. 31 St.
42	Fifth Ave. Presbyterian Church	5 Av. & 55 St.
6	First Church of Christ Scientist	1 W. 96 St.
43	Friends Meeting House	221 E. 15 St.
19	Fur Center Synagogue	230 W. 29 St.
16	Glad Tidings Tabernacle	325 W. 33 St.
45	Grace Church (Episcopal)	802 Broadway
2	Grace Church (Congregatioal)	310 W. 139 St.
30	Heavenly Rest, Church of the	2 E. 90 St.
11	Holy Trinity Lutheran Church	Central Pk. W. & 65 St.
31	Immanuel Evangelical Lutheran	Lex. Av. & 88 St.
47	John Street Church (Methodist)	44 John St.
46	Judson Memorial Church	55 Washington Sq. South
10	Lincoln Square Synagogue	200 Amsterdam Av.
17	Marble Collegiate Church	272 5 Av.
9	Metropolitan Baptist Church	236 W. 72 St.
40	Metropolitan Synagogue of N.Y.	10 Park Av.
28	Mount Olive Baptist Church	201 Lenox Av
39	New Church, The (Swedenborgian)	112 E. 35 St.
34	Our Lady of Perpetual Help (R.C.)	339 E. 61 St.
22	Our Lady of Pompei (R.C.)	25 Carmine St.
48	Our Lady of Victory (R.C.)	60 William St.
14	Radio City Synagogue	49 W. 47 St.
3	Riverside Church (interdenominational)	Riverside Dr. & 122 St.
38	St. Agnes (R.C.)	143 E. 43 St.
8	St. Bartholomew's (Episcopal)	109 E. 50 St.
42	St. George's (Episcopal)	209 E. 16 St.
21	St. John's Lutheran	81 Christopher St.
18	St. John's (R.C.)	210 W. 31 St.
5	St. John the Divine, Cathedral Church	1047 Amsterdam Av.
23	St. Joseph's (R.C.)	371 Av. of the Americas
15	St. Luke's Lutheran	308 W. 46 St.
44	St. Marks-in-the-Bowery	2 Av. & 10 St.
20	St. Mary's Church of the Byzantine Rite	246 E. 15 St.
29	St. Nicholas Russian Orthodox Cathedral	15 E. 97 St.
37	St. Patrick's Cathedral (R.C.)	5 Av. & 50 St.
24	St. Paul's Chapel of Trinity Parish	Broadway & Fulton St.
33	Temple Emanu-El	5 Av. at 65 St.
25	Trinity Church (Episcopal)	Broadway at Wall St.
35	United Methodist Church	150 E. 62 St.

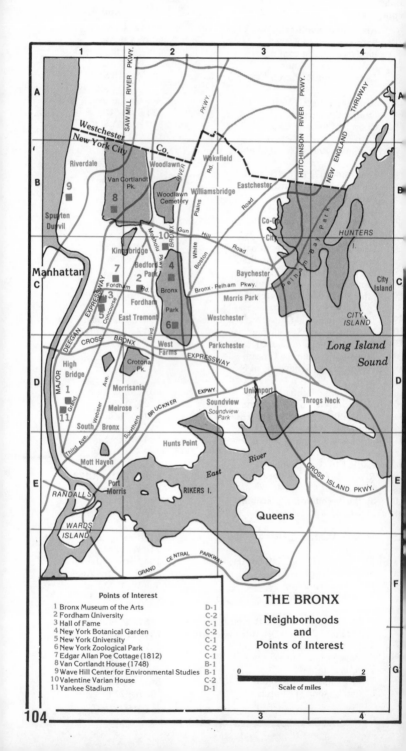

THE BRONX

Neighborhoods and Points of Interest

Points of Interest

1 Bronx Museum of the Arts	D-1
2 Fordham University	C-2
3 Hall of Fame	C-1
4 New York Botanical Garden	C-2
5 New York University	C-1
6 New York Zoological Park	C-2
7 Edgar Allan Poe Cottage (1812)	C-1
8 Van Cortlandt House (1748)	B-1
9 Wave Hill Center for Environmental Studies	B-1
10 Valentine Varian House	C-2
11 Yankee Stadium	D-1

0   2

Scale of miles

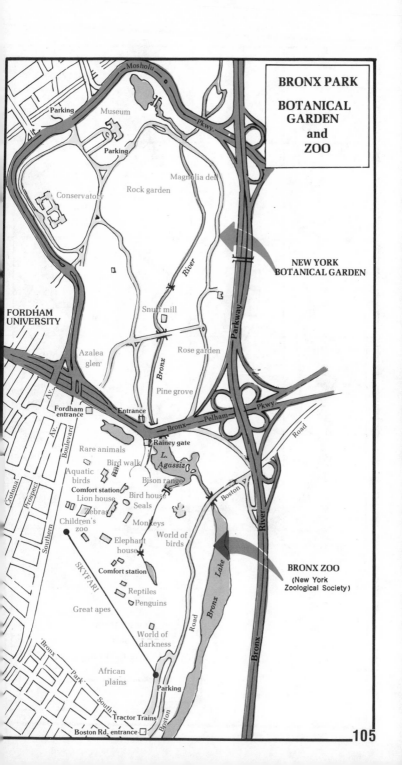

BRONX PARK

BOTANICAL GARDEN and ZOO

Mosholu Pkwy.

Parking

Museum

Parking

Magnolia dell

Rock garden

Conservatory

NEW YORK BOTANICAL GARDEN

River

FORDHAM UNIVERSITY

Snuff mill

Azalea glen

Rose garden

Bronx

Pine grove

Av.

Fordham entrance

Entrance

Boulevard

Bronx · Pelham · Pkwy.

Rainey gate

Road

Rare animals

Bird walk

L. Agassiz

Aquatic birds

Bison range

Crotona

Prospect

Comfort station

Lion house

Bird house

Boston

Seals

River

Zebras

Monkeys

Children's zoo

Southern

Elephant house

World of birds

Comfort station

SKYFARI

Reptiles

BRONX ZOO
(New York Zoological Society)

Penguins

Great apes

Road

Bronx

Lake

World of darkness

African plains

Bronx

Park

Parking

Bronx

South

Road

Tractor Trains

Boston

Boston Rd. entrance

105

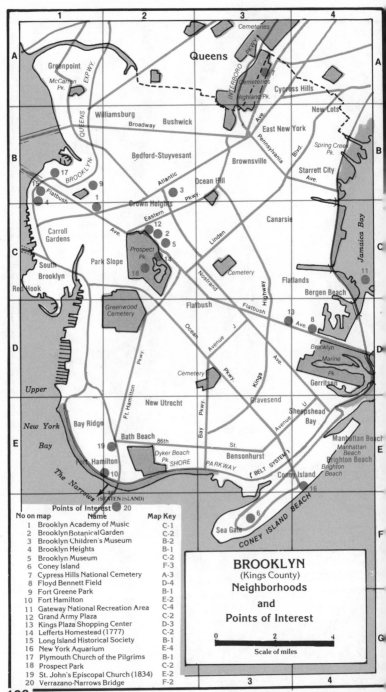

Points of Interest

No on map	Name	Map Key
1	Brooklyn Academy of Music	C-1
2	Brooklyn Botanical Garden	C-2
3	Brooklyn Children's Museum	B-2
4	Brooklyn Heights	B-1
5	Brooklyn Museum	C-2
6	Coney Island	F-3
7	Cypress Hills National Cemetery	A-3
8	Floyd Bennett Field	D-4
9	Fort Greene Park	B-1
10	Fort Hamilton	E-2
11	Gateway National Recreation Area	C-4
12	Grand Army Plaza	C-2
13	Kings Plaza Shopping Center	D-3
14	Lefferts Homestead (1777)	C-2
15	Long Island Historical Society	B-1
16	New York Aquarium	E-4
17	Plymouth Church of the Pilgrims	B-1
18	Prospect Park	C-2
19	St. John's Episcopal Church (1834)	E-2
20	Verrazano-Narrows Bridge	F-2

BROOKLYN
(Kings County)
Neighborhoods
and
Points of Interest

0   2   4

Scale of miles

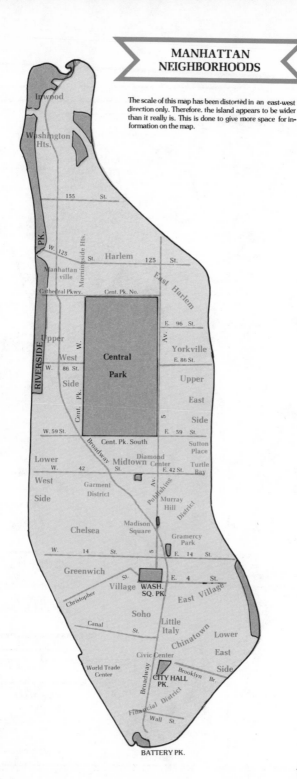

MANHATTAN NEIGHBORHOODS

The scale of this map has been distorted in an east-west direction only. Therefore. the island appears to be wider than it really is. This is done to give more space for information on the map.

Inwood

Washington Hts.

155 St.

W. 125 St. Harlem 125 St.

PK.

Morningside Hts.

East Harlem

Manhattan ville

Cathedral Pkwy.

Cent. Pk. No.

Upper

West

Side

W. 86 St.

Cent. Pk. W.

RIVERSIDE

Central Park

E. 96 St.

Yorkville

E. 86 St.

Upper

East

Side

5 Av.

W. 59 St. Cent. Pk. South E. 59 St.

Broadway

Lower

West

Side

W. 42 St. Midtown

Diamond Center

E. 42 St.

Garment District

Publishing

Chelsea

Madison Square

W. 14 St.

Sutton Place

Turtle Bay

Murray Hill District

Gramercy Park

E. 14 St.

5

Greenwich

Village

St.

Christopher

WASH. SQ. PK.

E. 4 St.

East Village

Soho

Canal St.

Little Italy

Chinatown

Lower

East

Side

World Trade Center

Civic Center

CITY HALL PK.

Brooklyn Br.

Broadway

Financial District

Wall St.

BATTERY PK.

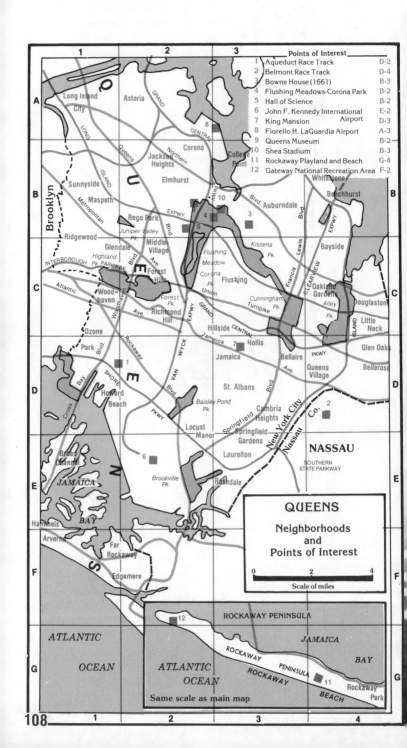

Points of Interest

1 Aqueduct Race Track D-2
2 Belmont Race Track D-4
3 Bowne House (1661) B-3
4 Flushing Meadows-Corona Park B-2
5 Hall of Science B-2
6 John F. Kennedy International Airport E-2
7 King Mansion D-3
8 Fiorello H. LaGuardia Airport A-3
9 Queens Museum B-2
10 Shea Stadium B-3
11 Rockaway Playland and Beach G-4
12 Gateway National Recreation Area F-2

QUEENS

Neighborhoods
and
Points of Interest

0 2 4
Scale of miles

ROCKAWAY PENINSULA

ATLANTIC OCEAN

ATLANTIC OCEAN

JAMAICA BAY

Same scale as main map

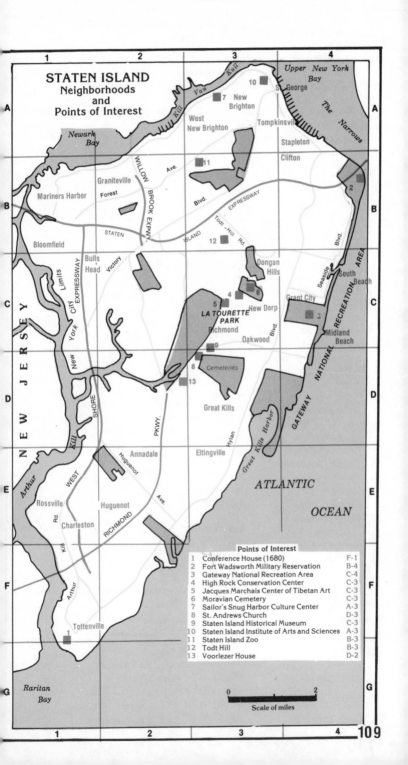

STATEN ISLAND
Neighborhoods and Points of Interest

Upper New York Bay

Van Kull

Kill

10

7 New Brighton

West New Brighton

Tompkinsville

St. George

The Narrows

Newark Bay

Stapleton

Clifton

11

WILLOW BROOK EXPWY.

Ave.

Graniteville

Forest

Blvd.

EXPRESSWAY

Mariners Harbor

STATEN

ISLAND

2

Bloomfield

Todt-Hill Rd

12

Dongan Hills

Blvd.

Seaside

South Beach

Bulls Head

Victory

NEW YORK CITY EXPRESSWAY

LIMITS

6

Grant City

New Dorp

3

Midland Beach

GATEWAY NATIONAL RECREATION AREA

5 4

LA TOURETTE PARK

Richmond

Oakwood

Blvd.

NEW JERSEY

9

SHORE

8

Cemeteries

13

PKWY.

Great Kills

Great Kills Harbor

Hylan

New

Huguenot

Annadale

Eltingville

ATLANTIC

Rossville

Ave.

Huguenot

OCEAN

Kill

Arthur

Rd.

Charleston

RICHMOND

Arthur

Kill

1

Tottenville

Raritan Bay

Points of Interest

1	Conference House (1680)	F-1
2	Fort Wadsworth Military Reservation	B-4
3	Gateway National Recreation Area	C-4
4	High Rock Conservation Center	C-3
5	Jacques Marchais Center of Tibetan Art	C-3
6	Moravian Cemetery	C-3
7	Sailor's Snug Harbor Culture Center	A-3
8	St. Andrews Church	D-3
9	Staten Island Historical Museum	C-3
10	Staten Island Institute of Arts and Sciences	A-3
11	Staten Island Zoo	B-3
12	Todt Hill	B-3
13	Voorlezer House	D-2

0   Scale of miles   2

The area code is 212

Emergency

Police, Fire and Ambulance, dial 911, or dial "O" (operator) for assistance.
Tell the operator, "This is an emergency call".
OR: call 628-2900, for Manhattan only.

For emergency when unable to reach your doctor	879-1000
Gas	683-8830
Poison Control Center	764-7667
Child Abuse and Maltreatment	431-4680
Rape Help Line	732-7706
Coast Guard	668-7936
F.B.I.	533-2700
U.S. Secret Service	466-4400

The New York Report (Official New York City Announcements)
976-2323

Other Services And Information

Abortion and Birth Control	966-3828	Metropolitan Opera	580-9830
Addict Assistance		New York City Convention and Visitors Bureau	397-8222
Air Pollution Complaints	966-7500	New York Public Library	790-6161
American Museum of Natural History	873-1300	Noise Complaints	966-7500
Better Business Bureau	533-7500	Nutrition and Diet	431-4540
Building Complaints	960-4800	Parking Violations	481-6360
Consumer Affairs	577-0111	Parks-Special Events	755-4100
Death Records	247-0130	Sanitation	925-2310
District Attorney	553-9000	Schools Information	596-5030
Health Department	285-9503	Sewer Complaints	966-7500
Heat Complaints	960-4800	Suicide Prevention	736-6191
Job Information	566-8700	Supreme Court	374-8524
Lincoln Center	877-1800	Subway and Bus Travel	330-1234
Madison Square Garden	564-4400	Sky Information Hayden Planetarium	873-0404
Marriage License Bureau	269-2900	Towaways	239-2541
Mayor's Office	566-5700	Transit Authority Lost Property Office	625-6200
Medicaid	594-3050	V.D. Information	269-5300
Metropolitan Museum of Art	535-7710	Water Complaints	966-7500
		Zip Code	971-7411

SPORTS

	(516) 794-9100	New York Knicks	594-6600
N.Y. Cosmos	265-7315	New York Mets	672-3000
Giants	20 1)935-8500	N.J. Nets	(201) 935-8888
N.Y. Islanders	(516) 794-4100	N.Y. Rangers	564-4400
New York Jets	421-6600	New York Yankees	293-6000

ALPHABETICAL LISTING